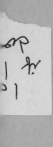

SMILE PLEASE

FOREWORD BY DIANA ATHILL

HARPER & ROW, PUBLISHERS

NEW YORK

Cambridge
Hagerstown
Philadelphia
San Francisco

1817

London
Mexico City
São Paulo
Sydney

Jean Rhys

SMILE PLEASE

An Unfinished Autobiography

"My Day" originally appeared in England and the U.S. in *Vogue*. British *Vogue* © 1975 by The Conde Nast Publication Ltd. U.S. copyright © 1975 by The Conde Nast Publications Inc.

SMILE PLEASE: AN UNFINISHED AUTOBIOGRAPHY. Copyright © 1979 by the Estate of Jean Rhys. Foreword copyright © 1979 by Diana Athill. All rights reserved. Printed in the United States of America. No part of this book may be used or reproduced in any manner whatsoever without written permission except in the case of brief quotations embodied in critical articles and reviews. For information address Harper & Row, Publishers, Inc., 10 East 53rd Street, New York, N.Y. 10022.

FIRST U.S. EDITION

Designer: Gloria Adelson

Library of Congress Cataloging in Publication Data

Rhys, Jean.
  Smile please.

  Bibliography: p.
  1. Rhys, Jean—Biography.   2. Novelists, English—
20th century—Biography.   I. Title.
PR6035.H96Z474   1980   823'.912   [B]   79–3666
ISBN 0–06–013602–2

80 81 82 83 84 85 10 9 8 7 6 5 4 3 2 1

Contents

It Began to Grow Cold

A Section of illustrations follow page 88.

FOREWORD

Jean Rhys and
Her Autobiography

JEAN RHYS began to think of writing an autobiographical book several years before her death, on May 14, 1979. The idea did not attract her, but because she was sometimes angered and hurt by what other people wrote about her, she wanted to get the facts down.

This was not the kind of writing which came to her naturally. When she wrote a novel it was because she had no choice, and she did it—or 'it happened to her'—for herself, not for others, in that it was at least partly therapeutic. She describes her first experience of the process in this book and it continued to work more or less like that . . . with the addition of a great deal of slow, meticulous and entirely conscious work which is not described in the chapter 'World's End and a Beginning' because on that particular novel (*Voyage in the Dark*) it was still to come. A novel, once it had possessed her, would dictate its own shape and atmosphere, and she could rely on her infallible instinct to tell her what her people would say and do within its framework. In a factual account she would have to rely on memory, not instinct, and this alarmed her. Her honesty was uncommonly strict, so she felt that the only dialogue she could use in such a book would be that which she was perfectly sure she remembered exactly.

Except in a few instances, how could she be sure?

A graver problem was that much of her life had already been 'used up' in the novels. They were not autobiographical in every detail, as readers sometimes suppose, but autobiographical they were, and their therapeutic function was the purging of unhappiness. Asked during a radio interview whether she had come to hate men, Jean Rhys replied in a shocked voice, 'Oh, no!' The interviewer said this surprised him, because most of the unhappiness in her life must have come from men. Jean answered that perhaps the reason was that the sad parts of her life had been written out. Once something had been written out, she said, it was done with and one could start again from the beginning. Much of the material she would have to consider in an autobiographical book had been disposed of in this way, so that raking over its remains would be unbearably tedious.

The solution towards which she slowly worked her way was that she would not attempt a continuous narrative but would catch the past here and there, at points where it happened to crystallize into vignettes. The stories in *Sleep It Off, Lady,* and their arrangement in chronological order, were an approach to this method, although it was only after they had been written that she saw they could be so treated. Three years before her death she began deliberately to pursue vignettes for the present book.

By that time she was eighty-six and old age was treating her harshly. She had a heart condition, and was quickly exhausted by any kind of effort, so that she could work only for an hour or two at a time, with long intervals between sessions; and her hands were so crippled that it was almost impossible for her to use a pen. A tape recorder seemed to her an actively hostile device, so there was nothing for it but dictating to a person—very difficult for someone as private as Jean Rhys. Fortunately she was able to find sympathetic helpers, none more so than her friend David Plante, the novelist. During the winters of 1976, 1977 and 1978, which she spent (as she usually did) in London, he devoted a great deal of time, tact and affectionate concern to taking down her words, typing them out, discussing them and reading them back to her for revision. She also accepted advice from him on the arrangement of some of the material. Without him she could not have completed the first part of the book as she did. Nor would she have begun to put the material for the second part in order.

The first part is the account of her childhood in Dominica, to which she gave the title 'Smile Please.' In it the vignettes link up, so that it amounts to an impressionistic picture of those years as a whole, rather than to scenes from them. And from the early part of the book's fragmentary continuation it can be seen that she was moving away from vignettes, towards continuous narrative, as she went on.

When I say that Jean Rhys completed the first part of her book, I ought to add that no sooner had she sent me the manuscript with a letter saying that it was finished at last, than she took the words back in the following letter: there was, of course, still some revision to be done on 'Smile Please.' We agreed, therefore, that when she came to London in about six weeks' time, as she was planning to do, we would go through it together so that she could give it the last touches. The fall which led to her death occurred two days before she was to make the journey.

I have no doubt that Jean Rhys would have altered a few words and cut others, but I am equally sure that they would have been very few. I can say this because I was her editor for *Wide Sargasso Sea* and *Sleep It Off, Lady,* and I have spoken to people who knew her when she was working on her earlier books. My own experience and their evidence leave me convinced that Jean Rhys allowed no piece of writing to leave her hands until it was finished except for the very smallest details. An example of her perfectionism: some five years after the publication of *Wide Sargasso Sea,* she said to me out of the blue: 'There is one thing I've always wanted to ask you. Why did you let me publish that book?' Here a gloss is necessary. She was a writer addressing her editor—a writer hampered by unusually beautiful manners. For 'let me publish' you must read 'badger me into publishing'—an unfair accusation, as it happens. I was indignant when I asked her what on earth she meant. 'It was not finished,' she said coldly. She then pointed out the existence in the book of two unnecessary words. One was 'then,' the other 'quite.'

I was not insincere when I apologized for failing to notice those words. Such an exemplary stylist as Jean Rhys has a right to demand infallible vigilance from an editor. So now I apologize to her for whatever unnecessary words there are in 'Smile Please'—although I would hesitate to remove them even if I noticed them, now that she is no longer here to give her permission.

About the second half of this volume, to which I have given the title
'It Began to Grow Cold,' I feel that apologies to Jean Rhys are less
necessary. This is because it consists of material which does not claim
to be finished and is not presented as being finished. It amounts to
being some, and only some, of what she wanted to say in the form
of first drafts, or notes towards first drafts. She intended to work on
it when she had rested for a while after completing 'Smile Please,' but
her increasing weakness during the last winter of her life prevented
it. One of the pieces was written with her own hand: 'From a Diary,'
which she had kept by her since 1947. She dug it out towards the end
of her work with David Plante, saying that she would fit it into the
book if she could see how. A small part of what she dictated is so
scrappy that it is confusing, and this I have omitted. Having available
two versions of some of the material, the second of which she had
agreed with David Plante was preferable to the first, I took the liberty
on one occasion—the passage on page 97 about accepting money—
of restoring a few words of her first version; I moved the joke about
actors and fish (page 89) to a position where it seemed to fit better;
and I quite often altered the punctuation resulting from the rhythms
of her dictation to something nearer the punctuation characteristic of
her other prose. Here and there—perhaps half a dozen times in all
—I deleted a word such as 'very' or 'quite,' so sure did I feel that Jean
would have done so had she been able to revise the passage con-
cerned.

  She did not get far enough with this second part of the book,
dealing with her life after her arrival in England at the age of sixteen,
to put the record straight in the ways she had intended. The reason
why it sometimes needs straightening is that because her novels are
so obviously autobiographical, readers suppose them to be more so
than they are. A typical example of this occurred in one of her obitu-
ary notices, where it was stated that her first husband, Jean Lenglet,
was imprisoned for robbery. It was Stephan Zelli in *Quartet* who was
imprisoned for robbery; Jean Lenglet was not. When the French
police arrested him in 1923 and extradited him to his native Holland,
he was charged not with robbery but with an offence against currency
regulations (in Jean Rhys's view, 'really very unfair because everyone
was doing it'), and with entering France illegally.

  What Jean Rhys used to say about the relationship between her life
and her novels only confirms what is understood by most writers and

students of writing, but perhaps it is worth recalling here. All her writing, she used to say, started out from something that had happened, and her first concern was to get it down as accurately as possible. But 'I like shape very much'—and again, 'a novel has to have a shape, and life doesn't have any.' If the novel was going to work, then it would soon start to have its own shape (her feeling seemed to be that the novel had it, rather than that she imposed it). Then she would be compelled to leave out things that had happened, or to put things in; to increase this or diminish that—all this to suit the shape and nature of the work of art which was forming out of the original experience. With Jean Rhys the process never took her a great distance from the experience—indeed, truth to its essence was vital to the therapeutic function of the work as well as to its value to other people—but it took her far enough to leave booby traps for the unwary. Mistakes made on the evidence provided by the novels may be hard to excuse but are understandable. Less so are wild guesses. In his biography of Ford Madox Ford, for example, Arthur Mizener has a note implying that Jean Rhys had a child by Ford. Jean had two children, both by Jean Lenglet: a son born in 1920, who died soon after birth, and a daughter born in 1922, who survives her.

That Jean Lenglet was the father of both her children is something which I know, from conversations with Jean, she wanted to say; and I can assume from other things she told me that it would have distressed her to see him described as a robber. What else she particularly wanted to include under the heading of record-straightening I do not know. I have, however, agreed with her daughter and with other close friends of hers that the short chronology on pages 149 to 150 will be a useful supplement to 'It Began to Grow Cold.'

A Note on the Publishing History of Jean Rhys's Books

This is a short version of a story which has often been told, included because newcomers to the work of Jean Rhys may find it interesting. She published five books before the Second World War. They were admired by critics but made little impression on the general public. After the appearance of *Good Morning, Midnight,* in 1939, she vanished from the literary scene (to which she never conspicuously 'belonged') so completely that people supposed her to be dead. By the end of the

war few people remembered her books; but one who did, Francis
Wyndham, worked for a time as literary adviser to André Deutsch,
Limited, and drew my attention to them. I shall never forget hearing
Jean Rhys's voice for the first time in the old copies of *Good Morning,
Midnight* and *Voyage in the Dark* lent me by Francis in—I think—1955.

It was Francis Wyndham who read in the *Radio Times* that the BBC
had been advertising for information about Jean Rhys, in connection
with a radio dramatisation of *Good Morning, Midnight,* and that she
herself had answered the advertisement. He obtained her address
and wrote to tell her how much he admired her work. She let him
know that she was writing a new novel, *Wide Sargasso Sea* (although
she had not yet found that title for it), whereupon he offered on our
behalf to buy an option on this novel. At that point—it was in May
1957—I wrote the first of the many letters Jean and I were to ex-
change. I proposed that after the publication of the new novel we
should, if all went well, reissue some or all of her earlier books.

Seven years went by before *Wide Sargasso Sea* was so nearly finished
that Jean Rhys was ready to bring it up to London and explain to a
typist the two or three very small alterations she still wanted to make.
It took so long because her husband had fallen ill and her life had
been so difficult that writing was often out of the question. I knew
from her letters how near she had been to despair, and I knew from
the batches of material I had seen on their way to the typist how
triumphantly she had prevailed over it, so the prospect of this first
meeting was a moving one. We planned to share a bottle of champagne over lunch.

Instead, we had to travel together to a hospital in an ambulance:
no sooner did Jean arrive in London than she had a heart attack.

She was to remain physically frail for the remaining fourteen years
of her life, and for the first two years after the attack she was so weak
and so despondent that she felt unable to do even the tiny amount
of work on *Wide Sargasso Sea* that still remained to be done. This was
a frustrating period for us, her publishers. We had in our hands the
manuscript of a beautiful novel which only its author could see to be
unfinished, but she had made me promise that I would not publish
it, or let it be published, until she had given her permission.

This she did at last because of a dream. She wrote to tell me that
she had been having a recurring dream in which, to her dismay, she

was pregnant. Then it came again, only this time the baby had been born and she was looking at it in its cradle—'such a puny weak thing. So the book must be finished, and that must be what I think about it really. I don't dream about it any more.'

Wide Sargasso Sea was received enthusiastically by the public as well as by the critics. It won the W. H. Smith Literary Award and an award from the Royal Society of Literature, and we followed its publication by reissuing all her earlier books except for *The Left Bank.* In 1978 Jean Rhys was awarded the CBE [Commander of the Order of the British Empire] for her services to literature.

Recognition came late—too late to give her much lively pleasure, although she was glad of the modest financial security it brought with it. Many of the forms it took were unimportant to her. The recognition an artist values most highly is that which comes from her or his peers, and Jean Rhys did not have many of those. One can only hope that at the end she drew private satisfaction from having so fully— to use her own phrase, on page 133—earned death.

Jean Rhys was also the translator of two books from the French. One was *Perversity,* by Francis Carco, published by P. Covici, Chicago, in 1928. The publisher named Ford Madox Ford as the translator, although Ford had secured the job for Jean. This made her angry at the time, but in later years she would speak of it quite cheerfully, saying that she supposed Ford's name would attract more readers than hers.

The other translation was *Barred,* by Edward de Neve—a pen name used by Jean Lenglet—published by Desmond Harmsworth in 1932. This novel and *Quartet* were based on the same set of events. Jean Rhys felt strongly about what was 'fair' and what was 'unfair'—words she used often. She told me she thought it 'only fair' that her husband's fictionalized version of events should be available as well as hers, and she took a good deal of trouble to find a publisher for her translation of it. She also said that she had given way to the temptation to cut a few—a very few—sentences about herself which struck her as 'too unfair.'

Diana Athill
May 1979

SMILE PLEASE

Smile Please

'SMILE PLEASE,' the man said. 'Not quite so serious.'

He'd dodged out from behind the dark cloth. He had a yellow black face and pimples on his chin.

I looked down at my white dress, the one I had got for my birthday, and my legs and the white socks coming half way up my legs, and the black shiny shoes with the strap over the instep.

'Now,' the man said.

'Keep still,' my mother said.

I tried but my arm shot up of its own accord.

'Oh what a pity, she moved.'

'You must keep still,' my mother said, frowning.

The chosen photograph in a silver frame stood on a small table under the sitting-room jalousies of our house in Roseau. It pleased me that it was by itself, not lost among the other photographs in the room, of which there were many. Then I forgot it.

It was about three years afterwards that one early morning, dressed for school, I came downstairs before anyone else and for some reason looked at the photograph attentively, realising with dismay that I wasn't like it any longer. I remembered the dress she was wearing, so much prettier than anything I had now, but the curls, the dimples surely belonged to somebody else. The eyes were a stranger's eyes. The forefinger of her right hand was raised as if in warning. She had moved after all. Why I didn't know; she wasn't me any longer. It was the first time I was aware of time, change and the longing for the past. I was nine years of age.

Catching sight of myself in the long looking glass, I felt despair. I had grown into a thin girl, tall for my age. My straight hair was pulled severely from my face and tied with a black ribbon. I was fair with a pale skin and huge staring eyes of no particular colour. My brothers and sisters all had brown eyes and hair; why was I singled out to be the only fair one, to be called Gwendolen, which means white in Welsh I was told? I was wearing an ugly brown Holland dress, the convent uniform, and from my head to my black stockings, which fell untidily round my ankles, I hated myself.

At the convent I had noticed that some of the girls' stockings were smooth, tightly stretched, and at last I plucked up enough courage to ask one of them how she managed it. She answered in that impatient, unwilling, secretive voice girls sometimes use to each other: 'Your garters are too slack.'

I borrowed a needle and strong cotton, went into the room where we left our hats and sewed a large tuck in each garter. Now, though not so smooth as some of the others', my stockings were passable. But as soon as I got home my mother noticed the change and objected so strongly to my wearing anything tight round my knees that I had to take the tucks out. Again my black stockings drooped.

After this I became one of the untidiest girls in the convent. Only one other was worse. She was Portuguese, called Gussie de Freitas, a most slovenly child and the despair of the nuns. Walking home down the hill away from the convent I would hear derisive shouts of 'Gussie, Gussie!'

Gussie had, like me, long straight yellow hair and eyes of my shape but black. She tried to make friends with me, perhaps she thought that outcasts should stick together, but I preferred being an outcast by myself and would have nothing to do with her though I took a perverse pleasure in trying to outdo her untidiness. I would lose my hair ribbon and come home with hair falling about my face and fingers stained with ink. If I wore a clean dress on Monday, by Tuesday it was spotted and creased. I was really rather miserable but took a defiant pride in looking worse every day. However, I always endeavoured to get into the house and tidy up a bit before my mother saw me. I was afraid of her.

I never looked at my photograph again but I often thought of it. Over and over I would remember that magic dress. It had been given to me on my sixth birthday, which had been spent at Bona Vista. But Bona Vista too had vanished.

When my father had been for a very few years in the small West Indian island of Dominica, he was optimistic enough to buy two estates in the hills (they were called estates then). Optimistic because, being a doctor, he spent his life working in the town and the districts near it, and neither of his purchases was a paying proposition. The larger of the two, Bona Vista, was very beautiful, wild, lonely, remote. From the windows of the shabby white house you could see a range of mountains: the highest, Morne Diablotin, then slightly lower Morne Anglais, Morne Collé Anglais, Morne Bruce. (In the French West Indies mountains are called Mornes and Dominica had once been French.) We believed, or I believed, that Diablotin was eight thousand feet high and that it had never been climbed because the summit was rock. Round it flew large black birds called Diablotins (devil birds), found nowhere else in the West Indies or the world. The top was usually covered in mist.

The other mountains were clear and we could see the rain coming and run for shelter before it fell. We were always there in August, the month of storms, much thunder and lightning, strong winds and heavy showers which lasted all day. Then, with the shutters closed, I watched the games played in the dim room, halma, beggar-my-neighbour, bezique or card castles. Sometimes it would clear suddenly and the sky was blue again. After it had rained, standing barefoot on the wet grass, the smell was unbelievably fresh and sweet. I shall never forget it. (We were not supposed to go barefoot on account of the jiggers, but we often did. Also it was our delight to eat with our fingers out of a calabash as the Negroes did. Food seemed to taste better that way. All this had to be done on the sly.) Below the mountains was forest, most of it virgin.

Our cook at Bona Vista was an obeah woman called Ann Tewitt. Obeah is a milder form of voodoo, and even in my time nobody was supposed to take it very seriously. Yet I was told about her in a respectful, almost awed tone. She was a middle-aged woman, tall, often smiling, which was unusual in a Negro. I can remember best her bare brown legs as, with her skirts girded up, she would carry dishes from the kitchen into the house.

The kitchen was a separate building, of course, and when it wasn't too smoky there I used to sit on a chest or a big box and have long talks with Ann. Or rather she would talk and I listened but what she talked about I haven't the faintest recollection. I think she told me my fortune, but I don't remember. When we left Bona Vista for the last time she saw us off still smiling, her skirt still girded high. As we never went back I've no idea what became of her, though I've never forgotten her, carrying dishes so carefully in the pouring rain.

It is at Bona Vista that I have my first clear connected memory. It was my birthday, the sixth. The upper part of the large living room had been cleared and made into a stage and my two brothers and elder sister were acting their version of Red Riding Hood.

I was wearing the new white dress, a birthday present, and a wreath of frangipani. A frangipani tree grew not far from the house; it was sometimes quite bare, even of leaves, then suddenly covered with pink sweet-smelling flowers. If you broke a branch it bled copiously, not red blood but white. Hibiscus, at least the hibiscus I know, fades soon after it is picked, but frangipani flowers last and are very easy to make into wreaths. The one I was wearing had been given to me first thing in the morning, and there I was crowned, bursting with pride and importance, safe, protected, sitting in a large armchair, my father on one side, my mother on the other, my shiny shoes a long way off the ground. My father had come up from Roseau for the occasion, a three-hour drive.

Suddenly my eldest brother, who was playing the honest woodcutter, if there is such a character, said in a bored voice, 'I'm not going on with this nonsense,' and walked off the stage. My second brother, always good-natured, jumped from outside through the open window, growling fiercely. He was the wolf and was dressed for the part in a long white sheet.

However, Red Riding Hood was silent, confused by the woodcutter's abrupt exit, and it was plain that the play couldn't go on. There was a large pale-blue book by the side of my chair. It was a birthday present from my father's mother, whom we called Irish Granny. She

kept track of our birthdays and all the way from distant England, or
Wales, or wherever she lived, I wasn't sure, books arrived. They came
at Christmas too, with boxes of chocolate, crystallized fruit, Carlsbad
plums, and a jar of Stilton cheese for my father. When the play
collapsed my mother picked the book up, opened it and put it on my
lap. Perhaps she feared I was about to cry. I looked at a picture of
a little girl in a pink dress. By her side was a huge spider and underneath meaningless print, for I couldn't read them, not even short
words. That's all I remember.

It was very shortly after that we left for Roseau. Bona Vista had to
be sold and we never went back.

Roseau. Family meals. The grandfather clock ticking. I was the youn-
gest, so I sat with my face to the pantry, watching the white tablecloth,
the low vases filled with corolita, the solid sideboard with the array
of pewter mugs and silver dishes and the picture of Mary Queen of
Scots going to her execution hanging above it.

Mary Queen of Scots was tall and stout, dressed in black velvet, her
right foot eternally advanced, walking daintily to extinction. The
crowd behind her was male, also dressed in black. I have often since
seen their narrow eyes, their self-satisfied expressions.

Beyond the sideboard and the picture of Mary Queen of Scots was
the door which led into the pantry. On the pantry table was a block
of ice wrapped in a woollen cloth. The safe had each of its legs
planted in a little cup filled with some sort of antiseptic to protect the
food from ants, like a baby's legs in badly fitting socks. There was the
knife-cleaning machine which my father had ordered because he
thought it a shame that a woman should have to do such bloody work
as cleaning knives on a board.

Sweet sugar stolen on the sly; frizzy hair . . . Victoria sitting on the
pantry steps grinding beans for the coffee after the meal, the delicious smell, for my father insisted on drinking nothing but mocha
coffee from his own land. The sound of cocktail-making, the swizzle-
stick and the clinking of crushed ice against the glass, which still
means the West Indies to me.

At Bona Vista there had been a telescope on the other side of the
house through which we could see distant Roseau Bay and the ships,
the Royal Mail, Canadian and French steamers, and sometimes a

stranger flying the yellow flag which meant there was an infectious disease aboard.

In Roseau we children played in the grounds of the old quarantine station, which were surrounded by a galvanized iron fence that made a satisfying noise when we rattled our sticks against it. Once the crews and passengers of infected ships were confined there, but now other arrangements had been made and it was empty and deserted, a favourite place for our picnics.

The gate was unlocked and it was easy to get into the large grounds but we hardly went into the big, empty house, and when I say empty, I mean empty. Not a broken chair was left, nor the frame of a picture, and the large rooms were painted a faded brown. There was nothing sad about the old quarantine station, though at one time many anxious people from suspected ships must have been herded there. On the surface at least it was a safe, bland, self-satisfied place, and yet something lurked in the sunlight. No one else ever visited it; perhaps it was supposed to be haunted. The real attraction for us was the children's swings which had been put up in the grounds. The seats were so broad and comfortable, the ropes so strong, not the most nervous child could doubt that swinging high in safety was possible. Swing, swing, singing:

> Soldier, soldier, marry me,
> With your musket, fife and drum.
> Soldier, soldier . . .

Life had changed a great deal for me since the days of the photograph. My two brothers had left the island for school in England and I never saw them again for many years. My eldest sister, a pretty and attractive child, went to live with one of my mother's married sisters in St. Kitts. Then she went with them to Nassau in the Bahamas. Soon it was obvious that she was no longer part of my life. I suppose she had been adopted but not in any formal way. My little sister was seven years younger than I was. She was now the baby, the spoilt and cherished one. I didn't hate her for supplanting me, indeed I remember feeling rather protective as I watched her walk unsteadily, but I think that my loneliness was very sudden. I was now expected to look after myself and the friends I played with weren't really important to me. I seldom saw the only one I really liked, Willy. He was now at school and taken up with the companionship of other boys. Gone were the days when we were all little, when we used to hop about together in a huge stone bath. Willy and his sisters, me and my brothers. We used to splash each other and shriek. Now I was alone except for books.

Books

BEFORE I COULD READ, almost a baby, I imagined that God, this strange thing or person I heard about, was a book. Sometimes it was a large book standing upright and half open and I could see the print inside but it made no sense to me. Other times the book was smaller and inside were sharp flashing things. The smaller book was, I am sure now, my mother's needle book, and the sharp flashing things were her needles with the sun on them.

I was so slow learning to read that my parents had become worried about me. Then suddenly, with a leap as it were, I could manage quite long words. Soon I could make sense of the fairy stories Irish Granny sent—the red, the blue, the green, the yellow. Then she sent *The Heroes, The Adventures of Ulysses, Perseus and Andromeda*. I read everything I could get hold of. There was the usual glassed-in bookcase at the end of the sitting room, but it was never locked, the key was lost, and the only warning was that we must keep it shut, for the books must be protected against insects.

I can still see the volumes of the *Encyclopaedia Britannica* that I never touched, a large Bible and several history books, yellow-backed novels and on the top shelf a rather odd selection of poets, Milton, Byron, then Crabbe, Cowper, Mrs. Hemans, also *Robinson Crusoe, Treasure Island, Gulliver's Travels, Pilgrim's Progress*.

My nurse, who was called Meta, didn't like me much anyway, and complete with a book it was too much. One day she found me crouched on the staircase reading a bowdlerized version of *The Arabian Nights* in very small print.

She said, 'If all you read so much, you know what will happen to you? Your eyes will drop out and they will look at you from the page.'

'If my eyes dropped out I wouldn't see,' I argued.

She said, 'They drop out except the little black points you see with.'

I half believed her and imagined my pupils like heads of black pins and all the rest gone. But I went on reading.

Meta

Now it is time to talk about Meta, my nurse and the terror of my life. She had been there ever since I could remember: a short, stocky woman, very black and always, I thought, in a bad temper. I never saw Meta smile. She always seemed to be brooding over some terrible, unforgettable wrong. When I wasn't old enough to walk by myself I can remember the feel of her hard hand as she hauled me along to the Botanical Gardens, where she was supposed to take me every afternoon. She walked so fast that I had to run to keep up with her, and most of the time, her face turned away, she muttered, curses I suppose.

She dragged me past Miss Jane's sweet shop. I'd often been there with my older sister before she left. Miss Jane was an old coloured lady whose small house was on the way to the Botanical Gardens and her sweets were not only delicious but very cheap. There you could get a small jar of freshly made guava jelly for a penny. The base of most of the other sweets was syrup—mixed with shredded coconut, a tablet, with ginger, a ginger cake. The most expensive were made of clarified sugar and cashew nuts. Those, I think, were threepence. The strangest was a sweet which was called lassi mango, if that is how it is spelt. When it was broken it would stretch indefinitely. The game was for one child to take one end, the other child the other, and go in different directions. At last it would be an almost invisible thread, and the joke was to watch someone walk into it and slap themselves, trying to account for the stickiness. Past all these delights Meta would drag me, taking not the faintest notice of my efforts to escape and jerking me if I looked back.

It was Meta who talked so much about zombies, soucriants and loups-garous. She was the only person I've heard talk about loups-garous (werewolves) in the West Indies. Soucriants were always women, she said, who came at night and sucked your blood. During the day they looked like ordinary women but you could tell them by their red eyes. Zombies were black shapeless things. They could get through a locked door and you heard them walking up to your bed. You didn't see them, you felt their hairy hands round your throat. For a long time I never slept except right at the bottom of the bed with the sheet well over my head, listening for zombies. I suppose someone came in and pulled it down or I would have suffocated.

She also taught me to fear cockroaches hysterically. She said that when I was asleep at night they would fly in and bite my mouth and that the bite would never heal. Cockroaches can be about two inches long, they fly and they smell very disagreeable, but it was Meta who taught me to be truly afraid of them. It didn't help that my mother, who tackled centipedes with great spirit, would go out of the room if a cockroach flew in and refuse to come back until it had been caught. Meta also told me that if a centipede was killed all the different bits would be alive and run into corners to become bigger, stronger centipedes. It must be crushed. She said 'mashed up.' To this day I'm not quite sure if I really saw two halves of a centipede walking away from each other, still alive.

Even Meta's stories were tinged with fear and horror. They all ended like this: 'So I went to the wedding and they say to me, "What you doing here?" I say, "I come to get something to eat and drink." He give me one kick and I fly over the sea and come here to tell you this story."

Years later I made great friends with a Negro girl called Francine. I've written about her before. Francine's stories were quite different, full of jokes and laughter, descriptions of beautiful dresses and good things to eat. But the start was always a ceremony. Francine would say 'Tim-tim.' I had to answer 'Boissêche,' then she'd say, *'Tablier Madame est derrière dos'* (Madam's apron is back to front). She always insisted on this ceremony before starting a story and it wasn't until

much later, when I was reading a book about obeah, that I discovered
that Boissêche is one of the gods. I grew very fond of Francine and
admired her; when she disappeared without a word to me I was hurt.
People did disappear, they went to one of the other islands, but not
without saying goodbye. I still think of Francine and now I can imagine other reasons for her complete disappearance from the house and
from my life.

More than anything else I detested a joke Meta used to play on me.
I became very friendly with a little boy who was called Willy, like my
father. When we came home from school we were supposed to
change into fresh 'afternoon clothes' as we called them. While I was
struggling with strings and buttons and hooks, Meta would say that
Master Willy had called for me and was waiting downstairs. I would
hurry up and fly down rather dishevelled to find no Willy and Meta
laughing loudly in the distance. She played this trick on me several
times before I became suspicious.

She was forbidden to slap me and she never did but she got her
own back by taking me by the shoulders and shaking me violently.
Hair flying, while I still had any breath to speak I would yell, 'Black
Devil, Black Devil, Black Devil!' I never dreamed of complaining to
my mother about all this, and I doubt if it would have been any good
if I had, but my relief was enormous when Meta left or was sent away.
I can't remember who took her place or if anybody did. But in any
case it was too late, the damage had been done. Meta had shown me
a world of fear and distrust, and I am still in that world.

Geneva

I KNEW LITTLE of the early life of my parents, how they met or why they married, and I didn't dream of questioning them.

I knew more of my mother for she was born in Dominica on what was then Geneva estate, and Geneva estate was part of my life. But I couldn't, or didn't, imagine her there.

Geneva was an old place, old for Dominica. I tried to write about Geneva and the Geneva garden in *Wide Sargasso Sea*.

My mother was a Miss Lockhart, a granddaughter of the James Gibson Lockhart who had arrived from Scotland at the end of the eighteenth century. He died before the Emancipation Act was passed and as he was a slave-owner the Lockharts, even in my day, were never very popular. That's putting it mildly.

It was during my grandfather's life, sometime in the 1830s, that the first estate house was burnt down by the freed Negroes after the Emancipation Act was passed. He was, apparently, a mild man who didn't like the situation at all and he died fairly young but not before a new estate house had been built, the one I knew. He left five children, twin girls of whom my mother was one, two boys and a baby girl called Edith. After his death the twins managed the place. One of the boys was old enough to take over when my mother married.

Whether old Lockhart (James Gibson) was as bad as he was painted, and exactly what happened, I was never told and never asked.

Geneva was perhaps a two-hour journey by horseback from Roseau and we children often stayed there. Not only the garden in the ruins, but the house itself, had a very strong atmosphere of age (though the house wasn't old), melancholy and adventure. I was happy there.

The steps down to the lawn. The iron railings covered with jasmine and stephanotis. In the sunniest part of the garden grew the roses and the 'English flowers.' But in the shadow the Sensitive Plant, which shut its leaves and pretended to die when you touched it, only opening again when you were well away. The gold ferns and the silver, not tall like tree ferns but small and familiar. Gold ferns, green and cool on the outside but with gold underneath which left an imprint if you slapped a frond on your hand.

Old Lockhart's portrait hung in the dining room. Was his hair powdered or was he wearing a wig? The painting had been saved from the flames of the first house, I suppose. Also his wife's. It was his wife, my great-grandmother, who interested me. I was told that she was a Spanish countess from Cuba but even then I doubted that. A papal countess perhaps? There were papal counts, I knew, so why not papal countesses?

She was pretty, with dark curls and a lively, intelligent face, and I tried to find out all I could about her from my granny, who of course knew her well.

After her marriage she was converted to Protestantism, Granny said: so a lapsed Catholic and according to the nuns, doomed to hell. On the other hand it was a sin to be sure that anybody was in hell, even Judas. Only God could judge. Perhaps there was hope and I was glad of that. I couldn't bear to think of my pretty great-grandmother in hell.

Granny was full of stories about her. She hinted that old Lockhart was jealous and suspicious, not only of other men but of her possible attempts to get in touch with Catholicism again. So that one day when she said smilingly, 'There was a lovely priest in my room yesterday,' an almighty row followed. It turned out that what she wanted to say was, 'There was a lovely breeze in my room yesterday.'

Granny lived at Geneva and so did her sister, my great-aunt Jane Woodcock who had never married. So did my mother's twin, Auntie Brenda whom we called Auntie B. It was a large house with room for everybody.

Granny sat sewing with a green parrot on her shoulder and if I ventured into her room the parrot would jump down, run along the floor and peck at my feet. At meals she talked a lot. Great-Aunt Jane smiled but hardly ever spoke; she seemed to be waiting to get back to her room and her patchwork. The lovely colours she used!

'Granny's castle,' I'd think, 'the castle of Great-Aunt Jane,' 'Auntie B's castle,' and far away, 'Uncle Acton's castle.'

At one time the estate must have been very prosperous but now, what with one thing and another, the profits were small and so was Auntie B's income. On top of everything else some of the Lockharts had made eccentric wills. One old woman left her large share to some young man she fell in love with in London, greatly to the Dominican Lockharts' annoyance. But it was legal and there is nothing to be done. That sort of thing ought to be stopped. Silly old fool! We never heard the whole story. Why was she a silly old fool? What ought to be stopped?

Auntie B lived very comfortably. She had a large cool bedroom, a big bed with a silk-cotton mattress, a dressing room which always smelled of Pears' soap, and a shelf of Rhoda Broughton novels, for she was the intelligent one. My mother preferred Marie Corelli.

One of my most vivid memories of my mother—she was sitting under the Seville orange tree at Bona Vista stirring guava jam over a coal pot with a wooden spoon in one hand and Marie Corelli's *The Sorrows of Satan* in the other.

Before I was old enough to ride to Geneva by myself (for horses were the only way of getting about then, mules and donkeys if you couldn't afford a horse, shanks' pony if you couldn't afford a donkey) Auntie B was accompanying me. About half an hour after we left Roseau she fell off her horse and lay still on the ground. I was very frightened for it was a lonely road and I didn't know what to do. Just as I was fearing that she might be dead and trying to nerve myself to find out, she got up, remounted and we rode on as if nothing had happened.

Every now and again she'd look round and smile at me in a reassuring way, though we didn't talk much. As soon as we arrived at Geneva she collapsed, was put to bed and the doctor was sent for. He said that she'd broken several ribs. After this I admired her, for it can't have been a joke, the long ride on that rough road with broken ribs. Yet she hadn't let me know that she was in pain nor said a word.

But I wasn't really a favourite. She thought me lackadaisical, too fond of books, I mooned about. Also I didn't like sewing and said so, which was a crime.

She led the procession to bathe in the Geneva river. The water was clear and cold with a strong current at the side. Lying in the current and being swept away, the loveliest feeling. Auntie B wore a sort of bathing suit or an old pair of drawers. We wore nothing.

But it was Granny's sister, Great-Aunt Jane, whom I adored. She let me sit on her knee, put her arms round me and kissed me. She came from St. Kitts and talked about 'beaux' and 'belles' instead of ladies and gentlemen. She had a black silk dress and a lace cap and wore her short white hair in ringlets as they used to do when she was young.

Once she made me, for a surprise, a cardboard dolls' house. Cardboard dolls with painted faces, cardboard tables and chairs, little tin plates for the dolls' meals. I was delighted and played with it happily though I never touched the wooden dolls' house in Roseau. There I liked the rocking horse with its flaring nostrils and its glass eyes. There were the piles of *Chatterbox* magazines bought for my brothers, and a jigsaw puzzle of the Capitol at Washington. Also several books warning us of the dangers of make-up. Strangely enough these were all American. I say strangely as one doesn't think of Americans as being very puritanical now. They described vividly your horrible and lingering death from lead poisoning if you used face powder. And other sorts of deaths, equally horrible, if you rouged or painted your lips. Years afterwards, as I slap make-up on regardless, I think I am still defying those books.

I loved Great-Aunt Jane better than anyone else in the world. Far better than my mother, even better than my father. Yet when the big quarrel came and we stopped going to Geneva I missed her very much at first but then gradually forgot her. Later on in England I heard of her death with scarcely a pang. She used to sing me old songs her mother had taught her but I've forgotten those songs.

The only time I went back to Dominica, long afterwards, I was told I must have a guide to visit Geneva.

I thought, 'A guide to Geneva for *me*? How ridiculous!' However, there was a guide, we went quickly by car and he seemed to know exactly where to take me. Where the house had been was an empty space; the Geneva house was burnt down two, or was it three, times. I stared at it trying to remember the house, the garden, the honey-suckle and the jasmine and the tall fern trees.

But there was nothing, nothing. Nothing to look at. Nothing to say. Even the mounting stone had gone.

When we got to the river I bent down and sipped from it. I was very thirsty and perhaps had some vague, superstitious idea that if I drank the water I'd come back. The guide caught my arm and said, 'Don't drink that. It's very dirty now. You'd be ill if you drank it.'

How many times had I drunk from that river when I was thirsty? There are supposed to be three hundred and sixty-five rivers in the island, one for every day of the year. Were they all dirty?

Yes, he seemed to think they were all very dirty indeed. 'Very dirty, not like you remember it.'

No, it wasn't as I remembered it.

The Doll

How OLD WAS I when I smashed the fair doll's face? I remember vividly the satisfaction of being wicked. The guilt that was half triumph.

Two dolls had arrived from England, a present from Irish Granny I suppose. One was fair, one was dark. Both beautiful. But as soon as I saw the dark doll I wanted her as I had never wanted anything in my life before. While I was still gazing my little sister made a quick grab.

'Oh no,' I said. 'Oh no, I saw her first.'

But when I tried to take the doll away she yelled and my mother rushed to her rescue.

'You must let your little sister have it. You don't want to grow up a selfish girl whom nobody will love, do you?'

'I don't care.'

'Silly. You ought to be pleased she's so happy.' Etc., etc.

'Now here's the fair one. She's just as pretty. Even prettier. And look, her eyes open and shut.'

'I don't like her,' I said.

'Don't be silly. Don't be selfish.'

With the fair doll in my arms I walked away.

'Where are you going?'

'Into the garden.' I walked out of the sun, into the shadow of the big mango tree. I laid the fair doll down. Her eyes were shut. Then

I searched for a big stone, brought it down with all my force on her face and heard the smashing sound with delight.

There was a great fuss about this. Why? Why had I done such a naughty, a really wicked thing?

I didn't know. I was puzzled myself. Only I was sure that I must do it and for me it was right. My mother was so uneasy that she spoke to my father about my extraordinary behaviour.

In his consulting room I stood and looked at him. I'd asked my mother once, 'What colour are his eyes?'

'Your father has beautiful hazel eyes,' she'd answered.

Hazel. A new word. I must remember that.

And now what? What's going to happen?

'What am I going to do with you? It was a very stupid thing to do,' he said, looking away.

'I wanted the other one. I saw her first,' I managed to say. 'She only wanted it because I did. It wasn't fair.'

'Nothing is fair,' he answered rather grimly. 'Nothing. And the sooner you understand that the better. You weren't very fair to the poor doll if it comes to that. So silly, so naughty. Why not give it away if you didn't want it?'

This was a new idea. Why not? No, that wouldn't have been enough.

'Your mother thinks that Great-Aunt Jane spoils you,' he said, still looking away. 'Encourages you to imagine that you must always get your own way or you will kick up a hell of a row. Perhaps you'd better stay here instead of going to Geneva next week.'

Not go to Geneva? Not see Great-Aunt Jane?

'Oh no, no!'

'Well, this time then. But you must not worry your mother like this. I will not have it. You must turn over a new leaf or I'll be very angry.'

But he hadn't told me why I'd done it and I thought he knew everything.

It was only in Great-Aunt Jane's arms that I could talk about it.

'They are always expecting me to do things I don't want to do and I won't. I won't. I won't. I think about it all the time. I'll never do it again.' (Never, ever.)

She said, 'Don't think about it any more.'

For the first time I wept for the fair doll. 'I'll bury her in the garden,' I sniffed. 'I'll put flowers on her grave.'

'Well now, that will be a nice thing to do,' said Aunt Jane.

'I can't imagine what will become of you,' my mother often said. And Auntie B doesn't like me because I hate sewing.

My Mother

I ONCE CAME on a photograph of my mother on horseback which must have been taken before she was married. Young, slim and pretty. I hated it. I don't know whether I was jealous or whether I resented knowing that she had once been very different from the plump, dark and only sometimes comfortable woman I knew. I didn't dare tear it up but I pushed it away to the back of the drawer. What wouldn't I give to have it now? Yet wasn't there a time when I remembered her pretty and young?

That must have been when I was the baby, sleeping in the crib. They were going out somewhere, for she was wearing a low-cut evening dress. She had come to say 'Good night, sleep well.' She smelled so sweet as she leaned over and kissed me.

She loved babies, any babies. Once I heard her say that black babies were prettier than white ones. Was this the reason why I prayed so ardently to be black, and would run to the looking glass in the morning to see if the miracle had happened? And though it never had, I tried again. Dear God, let me be black.

Even after the new baby was born there must have been an interval before she seemed to find me a nuisance and I grew to dread her. Another interval and she was middle-aged and plump and uninterested in me.

Yes, she drifted away from me and when I tried to interest her, she was indifferent.

One day, thinking to please her (this must have been long afterwards), I said, 'I'm so glad that you make our jam and we don't get it from England.'

'Why?' she said, unsmiling.

'Because I've just read an article about a jam factory in London. It was written by a girl who dressed up as a working girl and got a job there. She said that carrots, scrapings off the floor, all sorts of filthy things were put into the jam.'

'And you believed that?' my mother said.

'Yes, I do believe it, she saw it.'

'Well, I wouldn't believe a word a girl like that said. Dressing up to spy and then make money out of what you pretend you've seen. Disgusting behaviour!'

I said, 'Well, it wasn't so easy. She wrote that when she was dressed as a working girl men were very rude to her.'

'Serve her right,' said my mother.

One of her friends was a coloured woman called Mrs. Campbell. Her husband was a white man now retired from his business. Mrs. Campbell was kind, fat and smiling and I was very fond of her.

They lived some way out of Roseau. On this particular afternoon her husband wasn't there, and she took us for tea and cakes to a summerhouse which they'd built in the garden. There were no walls, only posts, and on these she'd hung sweet oranges (and our oranges certainly were sweet) cut in two and sugared. What seemed to me dozens of hummingbirds flew in and out as we sat there, their wings quivering as they hovered, sipping with their long beaks, then flying away again. I'd never seen so many. Mrs. Campbell was smiling at them when my mother began to cry. I had never seen her cry. I couldn't imagine such a thing. I stared at her more in wonder than in pity but I did eventually gather that she was crying about money.

'How could it stretch? What am I to do?' This is what I vaguely remember she said between sobs. I wondered if it was really money she was crying about.

Mrs. Campbell said, 'I have lived long and now I am old, yet never have I seen the righteous forsaken or his seed begging their bread.'

After a while my mother stopped crying and as we drove home in the trap she was her usual self-contained, withdrawn self. As I looked at her I could hardly believe what had happened. But this was the end of my comfortable certainty that we were not people who had to worry about expenses. For the first time I vaguely wondered if my father's reckless, throwaway attitude to money wasn't a cover-up for anxiety.

On certain mornings a procession of old men, no women, would come to the house and for some reason my father insisted that I must stand on the pantry steps and hand out the loaf of bread and small sum of money, sixpence or a shilling, I can't quite remember, that was given to each one. My mother objected strongly, she said they were old and often not very well, it wasn't a thing I should be expected to do. Truth to tell I wasn't fond of doing it.

One of them was very different from the others. He bowed, then walked away through the garden and out of the gate at the other end with the loaf under his arm, so straight and proud, I couldn't forget him afterwards.

> *Il y avait une fois*
> *Un pauvre gars. . . .*

My mother didn't argue any more but she arranged that we would leave Roseau two or three weeks earlier than usual. When we came back the bread and money had either been forgotten or someone else did it. There were no more arguments or processions of what the nuns called 'God's poor.'

Another memory. Sitting on the staircase looking through the bannisters, I watched her packing a trunk with blankets and warm things. One of the neighbouring islands had been hit by a bad hurricane and I don't suppose she was the only one to send all the help she could. I wonder if this happens now? I rather doubt it. I remember the expression on her face as she packed, careful and a little worried.

Just before I left Dominica she was ill and unable to come downstairs for some time. I went up to see her but walked softly and she didn't hear me. She didn't look up, she was sitting gazing out of the window, not reading, not crocheting or doing any of the things she usually did.

Behind her silence she looked lonely, a stranger in a strange house. But how could she be lonely when she was never alone? All the same she looked lonely, patient and resigned. Also obstinate. 'You haven't seen what I've seen, haven't heard what I've heard.' From across the room I knew she was like someone else I remembered. I couldn't think who it was, at first. Sh   out of the gate with a loaf of bread ur   l.

I wanted to run across the   :oo shy so it was the usual peck. Next   me downstairs and life went on as be

I think that she was happi   ·neva and came to live in Roseau. Thou   was often at the house. It was impossib   some link between them. One felt what the other was feeling without words. They would look at each other and both laugh quietly. This was often after one of my father's speeches about English politics.

He'd say, 'Oh, I do like to see them laugh like that.'

But I, watching, was uneasy. Could they possibly be laughing at me?

My mother was more silent but not so serene. Auntie B never lost her temper, my mother often did. My mother sewed beautifully but she could not cut out a dress. Slash, slash went Auntie B's scissors with a certainty and out of the material would appear a dress that fitted.

My mother could make pastry light as a feather.

Auntie B mixed famous punch.

Gradually I came to wonder about my mother less and less until at last she was almost a stranger and I stopped imagining what she felt or what she thought.

Black/White

I REMEMBER THE RIOT as if it were yesterday. I must have been about twelve. One night my mother came into the bedroom I shared with my baby sister, woke us up, told us to put on dressing gown and slippers and to come downstairs. We followed her half asleep. When we got into the sitting room my father said: 'Why do you want to wake the children up at this time of night? It's ridiculous.'

I heard far away a strange noise like animals howling but I knew it wasn't animals, it was people, and the noise came nearer and nearer.

My father said: 'They're perfectly harmless.'

'That's what you think,' my mother said.

I half realised that we had dressed to run away from the ugly noise, but run where? We could run as far as Mr. Steadman's house on the bay but long before we got there they'd kill us.

Kill us! This strange idea didn't frighten me but excited me.

They surged past the window, howling, but they didn't throw stones. As the noise grew faint my mother said: 'You can go up to bed again now.'

My father said: 'It was nonsense waking them up.'

My mother didn't answer, she only tightened her mouth in a way that meant 'You think one thing, I think another.'

Upstairs I didn't sleep for a long time. He thinks one thing, she thinks another. Who is right?

This particular riot was aimed at the editor of the local paper. His house was near ours. He had written an article attacking the power of the Catholic priests in Dominica. The crowd was some of the faithful who intended to stone his house, frighten him and prevent him ever writing about religion again.

However, I could not forget the howling sound and there's no doubt that a certain wariness did creep in when I thought about the black people who surrounded me.

The black people whom I knew well were different, individuals whom I liked or disliked. If I hated Meta, I admired the groom, liked the housemaid Victoria. She came from one of the 'English Islands,' Antigua I think, and was an ardent Methodist. As she washed up she would sing hymns in a low voice ('Steal away, steal away, steal away to Jesus'). She was sad and unsmiling and I was vaguely sorry for her and wished she was happier.

Josephine the cook was a Dominican. A tall, good-looking woman who kept herself very much to herself. I was rather afraid of her and so, I am sure, was my mother, who never went to the kitchen. They met in the pantry—neutral ground—and there she'd be given money to go to the market and buy food: fish, vegetables, fruit, sometimes meat. The fishing boats went out then, very early. Fresh bread was delivered by women carrying laden trays on their heads.

Josephine liked to be talked to in patois. Luckily my mother knew patois well. She was, in her way, a good cook. Her fish dishes were delicious, she made good curries, and often gave us crapeaux (frogs), crayfish, or stuffed crab. But I never liked her soup and she refused to make puddings. All the sweets from floating island to Christmas pudding were made by my mother.

I once peeped into the kitchen. It was very smoky and Josephine scowled at me. There were several people there that I didn't know so I never ventured again.

But it was the others I was wary of, the others I didn't know. Did they like us as much as all that? Did they like us at all?

The next thing that shook me happened at the convent. I was young and shy and I was sitting next to a girl much older than myself. She was so tall and so pretty, and she spoke in such a confident way, that she quite awed me. She had aquiline features, large flashing eyes and a great deal of not too frizzy hair which she wore in a loose, becoming way. She didn't look coloured but I knew at once that she was. This did not prevent me from admiring her and longing to be friendly.

My father was not a prejudiced man or he would never have allowed me to go to the convent, for white girls were very much in the minority. If my mother was prejudiced she never talked about it so I tried, shyly at first, then more boldly, to talk to my beautiful neighbour.

Finally, without speaking, she turned and looked at me. I knew irritation, bad temper, the 'Oh, go away' look; this was different. This was hatred—impersonal, implacable hatred. I recognised it at once and if you think that a child cannot recognise hatred and remember it for life you are most damnably mistaken.

I never tried to be friendly with any of the coloured girls again. I was polite and that was all.

They hate us. We are hated.

Not possible.

Yes it is possible and it is so.

My few intimates at the convent were white, among them three sisters from a South American country whom I greatly admired. I still connect them with angostura bitters though I'm sure their name wasn't Angostura. Their father was a papal count and this impressed me. I had no idea where he lived: Martinique, Paris, London? He was a tall, handsome man with a carefully trimmed beard, but his visits to his daughters were very few and far between. Once he came accompanied by a very pretty young white girl who he said was his adopted daughter. They used to drive about the Botanical Gardens in a smart trap and inevitably they were known as Svengali and Trilby. There was a burglary scare in Roseau and he bought two large dogs; they were called 'the count's Cuban bloodhounds.'

His visit over, the count would depart and from Europe postcards would arrive. I saw one: 'Study well, your loving Papa.' When Mother Mount Calvary talked about the girls or their father she always looked worried. I can't help wondering now if money arrived any more regularly than the count did.

Side by side with my growing wariness of black people there was envy. I decided that they had a better time than we did; they laughed a lot though they seldom smiled. They were stronger than we were, they could walk a long way without getting tired. Carry heavy weights with ease.

Every night someone gave a dance; you could hear the drums. We had few dances. They were more alive, more a part of the place than we were.

The nuns said that Time didn't matter, only Eternity matters. Wouldn't black people have a better chance in Eternity? They were Catholics and I envied their faith, for I was much attracted by what I saw of Catholicism.

The Corpus Christi procession passed our house and I watched eagerly through the jalousies. First came the priest, carrying the Host, then a procession of red-robed acolytes swinging censers. All along the way devout Negro women would erect little booths; sometimes they were very pretty to look at and the street outside was strewn with flower petals. At each of the booths the priest would stop and go in with his Host and the acolytes. What did he do in there, I wondered. What was it all about? I longed to know but never asked.

I would also watch through the jalousies as they passed the house on their way to Mass. They were dressed in their best, sweeping trains, heavy gold earrings and necklaces and colourful turbans. If the petticoat beneath the dress didn't make the desired frou-frou noise, they'd sew paper in the hems.

> *Frou-frou, frou-frou*
> *Par son jupon la femme*
> *. . .. . surtout*
> *Par son gentil frou-frou.*

Also there wasn't for them, as there was for us, what I thought of as the worry of getting married. In those days a girl was supposed to marry, it was your mission in life, you were a failure if you didn't. It was a terrible thing to be an old maid, on the shelf as they put it. The fact that I knew several old maids who seemed perfectly happy, indeed happier and livelier than the married women, didn't affect the question at all. I dreaded growing up. I dreaded the time when I would have to worry about how many proposals I had, what if I didn't have a proposal? This was never told me but it was in every book I read, in people's faces and the way they talked.

Black girls on the contrary seemed to be perfectly free. Children swarmed but Negro marriages that I knew of were comparatively rare. Marriage didn't seem a duty with them as it was with us.

All this perhaps was part of my envy, which rose to a fever pitch at carnival time.

Carnival

THE THREE DAYS before Lent were carnival in Roseau. We couldn't dress up or join in but we could watch from the open window and not through the jalousies. There were gaily masked crowds with a band. Listening, I would think that I would give anything, anything to be able to dance like that. The life surged up to us sitting stiff and well behaved, looking on. As usual my feelings were mixed, because I was very afraid of the masks.

Once when a friend of Victoria's came to visit her I was in the pantry. I was terrified of the way the visitor talked in a strange artificial voice with much rolling of the *r*'s. I was terrified of her mask. It was quite useless telling me, 'Don't be silly, it's only Regina dressed up.' I ran away crying.

Some of the men painted themselves either red or black and wore only loincloths. They would run along waving long sticks above their heads and jumping very high. They called themselves the Darkees or the Red Ochres. I used to think that if I met a mob of either Darkees or Red Ochres as I was going back to school after lunch, I would die of fright, but it never happened.

The only mask which I was not afraid of was called the Bois-Bois. He was not in a crowd but by himself, and he walked on high stilts and looked immensely tall. Before our house he would stop and do a formal little dance on the stilts and then I was sent out with sixpence or a shilling to give him. He would take the money, duck his head in a little bow, then stalk away to the next house to perform his little dance again.

I have watched carnivals on television. They are doubtless very colourful but it seems to me that it is all planned and made up compared to the carnival I remember, when I used to long so fiercely to be black and to dance, too, in the sun, to that music. The carnival I knew has vanished.

St. Lucia

WHEN I WAS about twelve years old, I went with Auntie B to St. Lucia.
I was to be bridesmaid at my uncle's wedding in Castries. Castries,
an exciting place. A regiment was stationed there, horse racing and
a lot of French people who gave parties and dances.

Passing Martinique, the Trois Pitons, Castries early in the morning.
Unlike Roseau Bay, Castries was a coaling station and harbour where
the ships came right up to the land. Little boys diving for money that
the tourists threw overboard.

The bride-to-be, Evelina, was pretty with a thick fringe and large
brown eyes.

We stayed in St. Lucia for about three months and it was a very
happy time for me. My aunt's warnings about fer-de-lances, a very
poisonous snake, and tarantula spiders, both supposed to be plentiful
in St. Lucia, didn't worry me. She had talked of my fear of the dark
and every night Evelina would come to my room and whistle to me
until I slept. She had a clear whistle, like a boy's. Of course I imitated
her, and began whistling myself. One morning Auntie B said: 'A
whistling woman and a crowing hen is fit for neither God nor men.'
She spoke to me but she looked at Evelina. Instantly I knew they
didn't like each other and they'd have to live in the same house.
Auntie B had always ruled supreme at Geneva. Breakers ahead, as my
father would say.

Staying in Castries for the wedding was a young man called Mr.

Kennaway. When he watches me I can see that he doesn't think I am pretty. O God, let me be pretty when I grow up. Let me be, let me be. That's what is in his eyes: 'Not a pretty little girl.' He is English.

The night before the wedding my aunt plaited my hair into many tight little plaits, so it should be wavy next morning. And it was. With my bridesmaid's dress, my wavy hair, and holding my bouquet, I looked at Mr. Kennaway when we met. But his eyes were just the same: 'Not a pretty little girl.'

My uncle was very much in love with Evelina. When he looked at her he had a rather silly expression, I thought.

After the wedding, when Evelina and her husband left for their honeymoon in Trinidad, we stayed on. Evelina's brother was like her but with red hair. He took me for long walks, showed me Castries, and one day asked if I would like to see a fight between a tarantula and a scorpion. 'We put them in a bottle and watch,' he said.

I asked who won.

'Neither wins. The spider bites, the scorpion stings, and they both die.'

But I didn't want to see the fight.

Cocks crowing, fine weather. The sea is so blue, I like this place, I wish I could stay here forever.

Then I was back home again but remembering the blue weather, the cocks crowing and Evelina whistling.

This stay in Castries was a definite stage in my life. It was the first time I had ever left Dominica or been on a big ship. If Evelina troubled to whistle to me every night because she knew the dark frightened me, she must have liked me. If her red-haired brother offered to arrange a fight between a tarantula spider and a scorpion, he too must have liked me. As for Mr. Kennaway, well, I needn't think about him. Some people were kind. By the time I left Castries Auntie B had made me some dresses I liked, a liberty bodice had been ordered for me from England, my stockings no longer drooped and I no longer thought of myself as an outcast.

The memory from St. Lucia of a long line of women carrying coals to the ship. Some of them looked very strained up and tired, carrying those huge baskets. I didn't like to think of them, but I hadn't asked any questions. I knew someone would say, 'They're very well paid,' and another, 'Yes, but women are cheaper.'

Soon after our visit to St. Lucia there was a big fire in Castries, and as all the houses were wood, it did a lot of damage. But as far as I knew it was built up again. I was very shocked when I heard someone recently, after they had made a trip to the West Indies, talk of Castries as a shanty town. I suppose they call Roseau a shanty town too, now.

I didn't know whether to answer 'It isn't true!' or 'We didn't do that!'

So, as usual, I said nothing.

As I had foreseen, Auntie B and the new bride didn't like each other at all. The time came when they quarrelled openly though we were never told why. Was it perhaps the pepper pot (meat preserved in red peppers)? The Geneva pepper pot was supposed to be one hundred years old. Perhaps the bride thought it time to throw it out. Or more likely it was the garden, which she may have found melancholy and decided to change.

In any case Auntie B left and came to live in Roseau. Left behind the silk-cotton mattress, the cool dressing room, packed, left and never went back. My father was very fond of her and thought she had been treated disgracefully, so we were never allowed to go back to Geneva. I never saw Aunt Jane again. What happened at Geneva I never knew.

After Auntie B left Geneva for good and for keeps she went to England, and I think Edinburgh, for a long time. When she came back she seemed a stranger. She never stopped talking about the theatre. She ceaselessly talked about the actors, the actresses and above all the scenery, which transported her.

She also bought a big hat with feathers on it. I remember it was pinned to the top of her trunk in such a way that the feathers weren't disturbed. She must have looked magnificent in it but I never saw her wear it.

I think Auntie B must have been rather accident prone, for after all this, when she came back she broke her leg. I went to see her, very nervous, and she said, 'Now then, don't look like dying Dick and solemn Davy, I'm not dead yet!'

But I was always a little nervous of Auntie B and couldn't muster up anything else than a rather forced smile. I think Auntie B was very brave, not like people are now. My mother was a quieter copy of her.

Poetry

I SKIMMED through *Paradise Lost* because I was curious about Satan. To me, and I think to most people then, Satan existed: the personification of evil, for some reason the ruler of this world. Satan was the enemy of mankind. He hated mankind and he was very clever in attacking it. He could be a very handsome young man, or he could be so ugly that just to see him would drive you mad. He was responsible for all the evil in this world and he perpetually made war on mankind.

So far as I could understand, everyone believed in Satan, and he was to blame for everything that had gone wrong. He could be pitiable, as in *The Sorrows of Satan,* or he could be terrible, the destroyer. In any case, for some reason he was all-powerful.

I read Byron because I hoped to be shocked, but I really thought of poetry as an examination subject. The way we were taught in our literature class didn't alter this opinion. 'Parse and analyse the following. . . . Point out the grammatical mistakes in the following. . . .'

Then, like a bolt from the blue, came Mother Sacred Heart, a new nun from England who took the literature class. Mother Sacred Heart must have been an ironical, sarcastic woman for I found her comments on Dominica and life in Dominica very unsettling. It was impossible not to know that many things I thought normal, even worthy, she thought highly ridiculous. I listened uneasily, half shocked, half pleased, wondering what else in Dominica she'd make fun of. But she very soon changed my opinion of poetry and poets.

She had a very beautiful voice and read aloud to us. She introduced us to Shelley and I soon stopped thinking of Shakespeare and company as examination subjects. I was able to make my own discoveries, even my own enthusiasms.

At the same time my father had arranged I should start extra lessons in French from Mother Mount Calvary. So as well as being assaulted by English poetry, I was assaulted by French poetry.

> *Beau chevalier qui partez pour la guerre*
> *Qu'allez vous faire*
> *Si loin d'ici?*
> *Voyez-vous pas que la nuit est profonde,*
> *Et que le monde*
> *N'est que souci?*

I was the *beau chevalier* of course, going far away, but I didn't hear a word of the rest of it. I still wonder why she taught me Victor Hugo's 'Un peu de musique':

> *Partons, c'est la fin du jour*
> *Mon cheval sera la joie,*
> *Ton cheval sera l'amour.*

Surely it was pitching my vague expectations rather high? Probably she thought it was an allegory.

When I went back to Dominica for a short visit the first nun I asked about was Mother Sacred Heart. I'm sure I did not imagine a certain reticence, even resistance, to talk about her. Well, she may have been an unruly nun but she was certainly a splendid teacher. I date all my love of words, especially beautiful words, to her half-ironical lessons.

Facts of Life

PLAYING IN THE BOTANICAL GARDENS, whenever I saw a group of the older girls standing together, talking with animation but in lowered voices, I drifted away. I didn't walk away, that would have meant being teased, but drifted slowly, cautiously, until I was out of earshot. I knew what they were talking about but I didn't want to hear. I was determined not to know.

Then one day I went into my father's empty consulting room. It was lined with books, brown and old-fashioned looking. I took a volume down. As it happened I opened it at a page where there were several diagrams of a woman having a baby. I was so horrified that I shut the book, put it back and avoided going into his consulting room again. As to the diagrams, I didn't believe them. Impossible.

Then my dog Rex, of whom I was very fond, had a love affair while I was taking him for a walk. I didn't feel I could desert him so I watched, horrified, and must have shown my horror because several passers-by laughed at me. I managed not to cry in the street but as soon as I got home I burst into tears. My mother came into the room to find out what was the matter. Unwillingly, I tried to explain what had happened and asked her, still sobbing, if Rex had some dreadful disease and was going to die.

'No,' she said. 'Rex is all right, never better.' Then she looked at me silently for a time. I think she saw the opportunity of enlightening me but she wasn't a woman to speechify and in any case had no speech ready. I'd taken her by surprise. She finally remarked: 'Well, don't cry about it,' and left the room without further explanation.

After this I shut away at the back of my mind any sexual experiences, for of course some occurred, not knowing that this would cause me to remember them in detail all the rest of my life. I became very good at blotting things out, refusing to think about them.

Gradually this withdrawal became curiosity, fascination.

I wrote this in my secret poems exercise book: 'Mr. Walton came to lunch today. After lunch he sat in a long armchair. He was so beautiful that I was afraid I'd faint.'

The older I grew the more things there were to worry about. Religion was then as important as politics are now. Would I insist on knowing more about Catholicism or would I stick to the English church? There was the business of black, white, not to say coloured. Had I ever really thought about it? Was my wariness justified? Or was my feeling 'this is not fair, not fair' nearer the truth?

There was also the business about ladies and gentlemen and that was terribly complicated and very important. It takes three generations to make a gentleman, I was told, or was it four? And though I didn't quite believe this I counted up the generations I knew anxiously. 'Nature's gentlemen' existed, but apparently no 'Nature's ladies.' That was probably right.

So as soon as I could I lost myself in the immense world of books, and tried to blot out the real world which was so puzzling to me. Even then I had a vague, persistent feeling that I'd always be l------ i-- defeated.

However, books too were all about the same thing, I di: but in a different way. I could accept it in books and fro (fatally) I gradually got most of my ideas and beliefs.

The old Victoria Memorial Library had been pulled d there was a new Carnegie Library in its place. It was very p   ....., usually empty. Sitting in a rocking chair on the verandah, lost in what I thought was the real world, no one could have been happier than I was. My one ambition was to plunge into it and forget everything else.

No one ever advised me what to read or forbade me to read something. I even looked at the rare and curious shelf but I don't remember any of it making much impression. I liked books about prostitutes, there were a good many then, and vividly recollect a novel called *The Sands of Pleasure* written by a man named Filson Young. It must have been well written, otherwise I would never have remembered it so perfectly to this day. It was about an Englishman's love affair with an expensive demimondaine in Paris.

I thought a great deal about England, not factually but what I had read about it. I pictured it in the winter, a country covered with snow and ice but also with millions upon millions of fires. Books, especially Dickens's, talked of hunger, starvation and poverty but very rarely of cold. So I concluded that either the English didn't feel the cold, which surely wasn't possible, or that everybody had a fire. Bill Sykes and Nancy, in fact, talked in front of a blazing fire. Cold: I couldn't imagine being cold but hated the word.

I'd fallen in love with other words, 'wisteria' for instance. I realised it was a creeper strong enough for the Wild Irish Girls to climb down from the dormitory window and escape to freedom and life. I was sure it had flowers; what colour? Red, no; blue, no; and not white. Favourite words, and words I loathed.

When years later I paid a short visit to Dominica I went to the library of course. Instead of being empty it was crowded, a long queue before the librarian's desk. At first I thought it was a very touching sight, all the black hands, eagerly stretched out, holding books. Then I noticed how ill the librarian, whom of course I knew, looked. As people filed past her she'd take the book, stamp it and give it back. No one looked at her and no one thanked her. They seemed to think that she was a machine and indeed there was something robotlike about the way she was working. Book after book and with each one she seemed to get more tired, look more ill. I wasn't at all surprised when I heard a few days later that she was dead.

I seem to be brought up willy-nilly against the two sides of the question. Sometimes I ask myself if I am the only one who is; for after all, who knows or cares if there are two sides?

As I grew up, life didn't seem monotonous or dull to me. Even apart from books, life was often exciting. It was not, of course, anything like as wonderful as England would be, but it did to be going on with. For instance, there were the horses. We had two, Preston and March.

On Saturday afternoons I nearly always went for a ride on Preston, the dark one. We'd race along the flat road past Canefields Estate and when Preston won I'd kiss his glossy neck, stroke his mane and say 'Darling, darling!' for he was a staid horse who allowed intimacies.

But then Auntie B bought a mare from St. Lucia and stabled her with us when she left for England. Her name was Irene, a pretty horse, but I was afraid of her long teeth, the look in her eye, and I never got beyond a discreet pat.

What is it about horses that makes you happy? It is so. Coming in from these rides I always felt that life was glorious and would certainly become more so later on (England, England!).

Other pleasures. My father's passion for cards was not satisfied with his games of bridge at the club. As often as twice a week there were bridge parties at home and I enjoyed helping my mother set out the green baize tables, the packs of cards, the ashtrays and the whisky and soda in the background. The ice, carefully wrapped, was kept in the pantry. At nine o'clock the old gun at the fort fired and I had to go to bed long before the guests came.

Then there were the musical evenings. Again the whisky and soda and ice, but who'd want to drink when they could listen to Mrs. Wilcoxon singing 'When We Are Married Why What Will We Do?' or 'The Siege of Lucknow'—that was Mrs. Miller. I didn't know where Lucknow was but I'd get very excited hearing about the sick Highland woman who heard the bagpipes of the relieving Highlanders before anybody else, 'The Campbells Are Coming' at the end, and my hands damp with emotion.

Before I was old enough to be allowed down during the musical evenings, I would sit on the staircase and look through the bannisters into a dark passage. Beyond was the room where the music came from. 'Night has a thousand eyes,' someone sang, and suddenly I don't want to listen any more but go up to my bedroom and undress quickly.

'Night has a thousand eyes,' yes, everything has eyes. Spiders have eyes, a good many eyes it seems if you look at a spider through a microscope. Moths have eyes, beetles have eyes, so have centipedes I suppose. Detestable flying cockroaches have eyes.

The window was wide open. It was so hot, so hot. So a cockroach might fly in. The cold stars look at me. 'Night has a thousand eyes'; more like a million I think.

My little sister was asleep in the crib, the crib that once I lay in. What would be the good of her, even if I did wake her up? Better to pull the sheet over my head and hide. 'Night has a thousand eyes.'

As for my little sister, it's curious how little I remember of her. She was too young to be a companion, old enough for me to guess she never would be.

She was an extrovert. Almost as soon as she started growing up she seemed to have many friends. It seemed she did all she was expected to do and nothing that she wasn't. I think I was fond of her in a vague sort of way, but we were never close.

I remember her best much later on when, rather unwillingly, she was one of the company with whom I did my plays. I think that this bored her and the fact that she was always the princess and I didn't mind being the wicked old baron didn't interest her.

She had a sweet face.

My Father

My FATHER'S SISTER, who was called Clarice, spent the winter in the West Indies with us three times. The first time I was too young to remember, or perhaps I wasn't born. The third time she came to take me back to England. The second time she stayed several months and it was mostly from her talk that I pieced together something of my father's life.

I knew that he was the son of an Anglican clergyman, the rector of a small village in Wales, of which I could never remember the name. I also knew vaguely that he had run away to sea. But it was Aunt Clarice who described how he was caught at Cardiff and taken back to the rectory. At this time he wasn't quite fourteen. Apparently he persisted that he wanted to spend his life as a sailor, and he was sent to the training ship *Worcester*. When he left he got a job on a sailing ship. At the end of that voyage he went home unwillingly to the rectory. I only heard him speak once of the sailing voyage on which he was so unhappy, and I remembered it. The captain seems to have been a very brutal man who said, 'I'll teach you to think you're a gentleman.' However, as my father didn't like his father he was even more unhappy at home.

There was a photograph of an old man with a clerical collar in the sitting room in Roseau. One day I came in unexpectedly and saw him standing in front of the photograph shaking his fist and cursing. My mother's version of this was: 'The old man grudged every penny spent on Willy. Everything must go to the eldest son, his favourite.'

When he decided to become a doctor it was his mother who found the money. As soon as he had qualified he got a job as a ship's doctor.

When other children boasted of rich or distinguished relatives in England I used to say that my father had been to every country in the world. He had certainly been to a good many. I knew nothing of his life then for several years. Why he came to Dominica when he was nearly thirty, how he met my mother, all that I didn't know. It was Aunt Clarice who told me he had fallen very ill with fever after he'd accepted a Government post in Dominica. He wasn't in Roseau then, his district was close to Geneva Estate, and when the twins heard of his illness they came over and nursed him back to health. As soon as he recovered he married my mother. This is more or less what I was told anyway, or gathered.

As I remember him he was a man of middle height with broad shoulders and a great deal of grey wavy hair. Every now and again he would go to the barber's and have it cut so short you could see his scalp. I hated him then, and had to force myself to kiss him good night, but it soon grew again. He had a red moustache, not a Kaiser Bill, not a Hitler, not a Zapata, but a kind moustache.

It was also my Aunt Clarice who first gave me the idea that he was a sad man, continually brooding over his exile in a small Caribbean island. This was the contrary of what I had thought before.

The entrance to the house was a long passage which we called the gallery. It was empty except for a wicker sofa, and at the end a round table with a green-shaded reading lamp, the latest *Times* weekly edition, a fortnight old, his pipe rack, and a large armchair where he sat reading and we weren't allowed to disturb him or speak to him. He was supposed to be reading, but was he reading? It was after Aunt Clarice's revelations that I wondered if he was gathering up strength to appear happy, jolly. 'Poor Willy,' she would say meaningly. 'Poor, poor Willy.'

Needless to say, my mother and my aunt disliked each other, though they were always extremely polite. Something about Aunt Clarice made me uneasy. Her long fingers were not pretty but frightening. The meaning behind things she'd say I guessed at, so that when I was told I was to go to England with her, to school, I was not altogether happy. When I think about her now I am still quite undecided. I don't know whether she was a kind but suppressed woman who bore with me as long as she could for her brother's sake, or a cool sarcastic person who disapproved of me from the first and was delighted to get rid of me at the first opportunity.

To her credit it must be said that later on, in London, when she came to fetch me at my first rehearsal of *Our Miss Gibbs,* all the girls were delighted with her. 'Is this your Auntie, oh isn't she nice!'

It was Aunt Clarice who told me about the legendary Aunt Jeanette. She had been a great beauty married to a professor of mathematics at Cambridge University. He was much older than she was, untidy, unattractive and so absent-minded he was a joke, appearing for lectures dressed in his pyjamas. They were known as Beauty and the Beast.

When I went to England I was for a short time in Cambridge. On Saturday afternoons I would go to tea with Aunt Jeanette, who lived somewhere in the Trumpington Road. She was still very beautiful and had, like other ladies of that time, a devoted maid. I was afraid of the maid, who always let me in with a tight mouth and suspicious eyes. In the armchair in the sitting room Aunt Jeanette would be seated, beautifully dressed, her hair just so, her lovely hands almost transparent when she held them up to the fire. I was rather uneasy but I knew I was privileged.

One afternoon while we were sipping tea she asked me, 'Have you ever read the Song of Songs?'

I said, 'You mean in the Bible? Yes, I have read it.'

'I hope,' she said, rather severely, 'that you don't imagine it's about a woman. Or about a man's feelings for a woman. It's an allegory of the relationship of Christ and His church.'

'But, Aunt Jeanette,' I said, 'Christ wasn't born when Solomon wrote that.'

'A prophetic allegory,' she said. 'Great poems are often allegories. There's meaning behind the meaning.'

'Is Omar Khayyam an allegory too?' I asked. At that time I was very fond of Omar Khayyam.

'Oh no, that's not an allegory. That's just a bad translation.'

'I like it anyway,' I said.

'I daresay. But people who ought to know tell me that FitzGerald's translation is a very inaccurate one indeed.'

My Saturday teas with Aunt Jeanette were rather awe-inspiring but certainly weren't dull. I used to hear all the Cambridge gossip of her day.

'Poor Darwin. He has threaded the labyrinths of creation and lost his creator,' etc., etc.

I rarely found her anything but fascinating. I was very astonished when, one of the last times I saw her, she embraced me and kissed me and said, 'Poor lamb, poor lamb.' Perhaps she knew that I was bound for a stormy passage and would be seasick most of the time.

I'm sure now that Aunt Clarice was wrong about my father. He wasn't a sad man. He was an active, outgoing man with many friends. He was sad when his mother died, so sad that his sadness filled the house. He didn't even pretend to read then. When a friend arrived my father looked at him and said, 'She's dead.' 'Who's dead?' said the friend. My father didn't answer, and the friend went into the sitting room, where my mother explained that he had had very bad news.

That was Irish Granny, so there were no more presents at Christmas, no more books. Her last present to me was a novel about Richard Brinsley Sheridan and his love for Elizabeth Lindley, a singer. I suppose this was to let me know she realised I was growing up.

I probably romanticised my father, perhaps because I saw very little of him. School at the convent started early, at eight o'clock. We usually woke at about six and were having breakfast at seven, but with my mother. It was a delicious breakfast with good coffee and hot rolls bought that morning. They made good bread at that time, not croissants but petits pains, which you split down the middle to let the butter melt into the centre. By half past seven I was on my way to the convent. My father woke and breakfasted a good deal later, about nine o'clock. He had what my mother called an English breakfast but it was only a boiled egg. After breakfast he'd set out for one of his districts, in the trap if the road was good enough, on horseback otherwise. He usually lunched with a friend or with the local priest. He was the doctor for the presbytery and for the convent. When he came back we were again at school. I suppose he saw private patients in the afternoon, or they came to him. As soon as the day's work was over he'd go up to the club to play bridge, for cards were his passion.

For a time dinner was a family meal, and I saw my father there. My mother would listen by the hour to him holding forth about English politics and getting very excited, but she never gave an opinion. All my mother would say after sidelong glances at us was, 'Don't do that!' We discovered that we could play tunes on the finger bowls. The exciting thing was that each finger bowl gave off an entirely different note and again a different note if you put the finger bowl on a table napkin. Was it the amount of water that mattered? I longed to experiment but never could, for after meals they were put away.

My father never seemed to notice us at all, far too engaged in either abuse or praise of various English politicians, while my mother watched us the whole time. Soon we weren't allowed to dine with the grownups, especially when there were guests, because it was decided we were nuisances. That was my father's life as I knew it, and I still think he enjoyed it, or part of it.

I remember his always being very kind and gentle to me. It was he who stopped the hated plate of porridge my mother suddenly expected me to eat every morning, and arranged that I should have an egg beaten up in hot milk with nutmeg instead. He who stopped the extra lessons in mathematics when he found me crying because I could never understand it.

His habit of listing his various friends (I suppose to reassure himself) and his long speeches about English politicians were boring, but I didn't find them so.

I can only remember my father in little things. I can remember him walking with me arm in arm up and down the verandah, how pleased I was. He gave me a coral brooch and a silver bracelet.

One of my last memories of him was with a woman who had spent most of her life in India. She was small and thin and burnt brown. They must have been talking about religion, about Buddhism, for she said, 'What's the use of living hundreds and hundreds of lives merely to end up in nothingness?' He said, 'But Nirvana is not nothingness. Nirvana is . . .'

I've forgotten how he explained Nirvana.

I felt, or knew at once, that my father liked women. Some of the men I came across didn't, I knew that too. For instance, Mr. Kennaway. But talking to women, especially pretty ones, my father had a gentler, teasing way. You saw that he liked them. Also he would flirt outrageously with anyone attractive who came to the house. My mother didn't seem to mind at all and now I wonder if she minded but didn't show it.

It still seems strange to me that he's dead. I heard the other day that the Celtic cross my mother put up so proudly over his grave had been knocked down and his grave wasn't marked any more. I hated whoever had done this and thought, 'I can hate too.'

Sundays

EVEN ON SUNDAYS we didn't see much of my father. Sunday always seemed to be fine. That was God's doing, I used to think. Also very hot so that it was difficult to stand still while the sash to my white dress was tied at the back. I had two sashes, a pink and a blue. In the hottest part of the day we would set out and climb the hill to the Anglican church. My father never was there on these occasions but it was understood that he must rest on Sundays and we never questioned that.

Most of the time at church, especially during the litany, I was bored stiff. Bored, though I didn't know the word, only the feeling as Mr. Dance droned on and the thin hassocks we knelt on grew thinner and our knees began to hurt. Sometimes I would think of some of the various parodies on the litany that began 'Stir up, we beseech Thee': 'Stir up we beseech Thee a pudding sweet and hot, and grant we beseech Thee that I may get a lot.' Then my mind would go back to what the clergyman said: 'By Thy agony and bloody sweat, by Thy cross and passion . . .'

It was too hot in that church. Even my mother, who never felt the heat, fanned herself ceaselessly with a large palm leaf fan. The pew near us across the aisle was occupied by a Mr. Burton, his wife and two children. They never knelt because Mr. Burton disapproved of kneeling. He said it was papist, and that he wouldn't kneel to anybody or anything. So when the rest of the congregation knelt, they all sat

at the extreme edge of their seats, in a crouching position, heads
bent, eyes shut. It looked very uncomfortable and when everyone was
able to sit up, Mr. Burton looked hot and red. However, he soon
recovered enough to keep a wary eye on Mr. Dance, the clergyman,
whom he suspected of wanting to introduce other papist practices,
genuflexion, incense, then confession, and the door wide open to the
Great Whore of Babylon. As to the worship of the Virgin Mary,
'Worship a woman,' Mr. Burton would say. 'I'd as soon worship a
bloody cow!' The High Church members of the congregation bowed
low at the name of Jesus and faced to the east at the time of the Creed.

In front of us sat the three Miss Porters. The small one in the
middle, the other two guarding her. The small Miss Porter had once
been the heroine of a great scandal. She had become engaged to a
young visiting Englishman and was very much in love with him. She
showed her ring to everyone and said that after the marriage they
would live in England (what bliss!). She was rather nervous about
meeting his family, she said, but he was *such* a kind man, his family
was certain to be kind too. Then Geoffrey—that was the young Englishman's name—disappeared. Without a word of explanation to anyone he booked his passage on the Royal Mail to Southampton. At first
Miss Jessie wouldn't believe it.

'He must have had bad news. A letter will come explaining everything.'

But weeks, then months, passed and no letter came. At first everyone sympathised. A shameful way to treat a girl, shameful! Unfortunately, men are not to be trusted. However, when it became known
how she behaved when she finally gave up hope, opinions differed.
She tore down Queen Victoria's picture, broke the glass then spat on
it, stamped on it, at last tore it up, using the most violent language
all the time (you wouldn't believe the words she knew, the servants
said). Then she became very ill, and a bit of a nuisance too, everybody
said. If she'd behaved like poor Jenny Dixon who after a similar
experience had quietly gone to bed and died, or Rosemary Acton who
hadn't cared a bit and married someone else . . . each in her own way
was admirable. Miss Jessie decidedly not. Some people even said that
Geoffrey had had a glimpse of her violent temper and fled. In any case
years afterwards there she was in the pew in front. The curious thing
was that after all this time her face was still pretty, almost unwrinkled.

But she didn't look young. Not at all. Twisted somehow. Also she hardly ever spoke unless spoken to, and had a way of staring in front of her at nothing.

'Miss Jessie isn't all there,' people said.

'Then where is she?' I asked one day.

'It's only a saying,' my mother said.

There are other people I remember. Mrs. Jarvis had huge brown eyes, so melting, so sad, so imploring, changing so quickly to a sharply curious look when she studied another woman. She was one of the sheep who look up and are not fed. Why are her eyes so different? She was very thin and the doctor told her that during the hot part of the day she mustn't just rest as most people did, but undress, go to bed and try to sleep. But always she got thinner, her eyes more hungry and inquisitive. Mr. Jarvis I cannot remember at all.

Then there was Mr. Porter, tall, also very thin, a freethinker as they were called then, a vegetarian and a socialist. I do not remember a Mrs. Porter.

Mr. Scully ate nothing but fruit.

The Religious Fit

WHEN I FIRST KNEW I was to be sent to the convent as a day scholar I was very frightened. I cried, shrieked, clung to my mother and kicked up such a fuss that I didn't go. This wasn't altogether my fault. There was a certain prejudice against Catholicism among the white people and I'd heard many horror stories about the nuns. Also most of the girls at the convent were coloured, that is of mixed blood, another reason for general surprise at my going there. The day after my screaming fit I was taken to the convent, most unwillingly. I didn't like the two lay sisters whom I saw first, but the other nuns and most of the girls were kind and soon I became reconciled to it.

I know how memory exaggerates but I still think it was a large, cool, green place. There were three houses. First the house where the nuns lived; the chapel was there, also the room where the Mother Superior received her visitors and two small cubicles with pianos where those of us who had lessons in music practised.

It was quite a long walk to the second house, through fairly large grounds. Two big trees and a lot of green space. Here were our classrooms, with the dormitories on the second floor, a stone bath outside and another room where we ate. By the side of this was the black children's school. We used to hear them singing their tables: 'Twice one is two, twice two is four . . .'

Attending the catechism lessons or listening to the lives of the saints being read aloud while we were doing needlework slid off me.

But I liked the Catholic catechism better than the Anglican.

'What is your name?' 'L or M.' I wasn't L and I wasn't M. It didn't apply to me. 'Who gave you this name?' 'My godfather and god-mother in my baptism.' I didn't even know my godfather's name. There was a silver mug on the sideboard which he had given me as a ritual gift before he left the island, called 'Gwen's mug.'

So I preferred the Catholic catechism, which was much more forth-right. 'Who made you?' it asked, and my chief memory of the cate-chism was a little girl who persisted obstinately in saying, 'My mother!'

'No, dear, that's not the answer. Now think—who made you?'

'My mother,' the stolid girl replied. At last the nun, exasperated, banished her from the class.

We prayed for the souls in purgatory every day. I heard about hell.

Mother Mount Calvary, the Superior, was a cheerful woman with large brown eyes and a rosy face. She gave me extra lessons in French and music so I saw a lot of her and grew to love her.

Mother St. Joseph was the only coloured nun except for the two lay sisters in the kitchen. She was very beautiful. Even then I could see that. Her dark face, with huge dark eyes, was framed in white linen. She taught history and for a while vanished. When she reap-peared she seemed thinner than I remembered, but she smiled at us very sweetly and the lesson began. It wasn't a very hot day and she was sitting near the open window, but I soon noticed that large drops of sweat rolled down her forehead which now and again she mopped with a handkerchief. Her voice too had changed and the lesson was shorter than usual. I was very shocked when, coming away, one of the girls said casually, 'Mother St. Joseph is dying.' I thought that only old people died, or people who had been very ill, accidents of course, not people whom you'd just seen and talked to. I jumped as high as I could and ran very fast. Dying? No, not me, never! The whole thing seemed to me unfair, and probably untrue. We never saw Mother St. Joseph again.

When my father, after working for twenty-five years in Dominica, was given his first leave, I was quite happy at the idea of becoming a boarder at the convent. It may have been for six months or a year. I forget. He spent it in England and took my mother with him. They made other plans for my little sister.

It had all along been understood that I was not to be pressured into Catholicism, and I wasn't. But there was a disadvantage to this: I was never allowed to go into the chapel, nor was I taken to Mass. However, twice I went to the service they called Benediction.

The Roseau cathedral was much larger than the Anglican church and I'd always heard it was a hideous place, worse than the Anglican which was bad enough. But when I went into it I thought it beautiful. Instead of the black people sitting in a different part of the church, they were all mixed up with the white and this pleased me very much. I thought it right. Of course, very few of the white people were Catholics but there were some Irish families on the island and the occasional tourist.

I was fascinated by the service, the movements of the priest, the sound of Latin, the smell of incense. It wasn't long before I decided firmly that I would become a Catholic, and not only a Catholic but a nun. I thought of the convent as a safe place—there I would live happily (but not for too long), the bride of Christ, my place in heaven secure. If I got anxious or doubtful there would always be Mother Mount Calvary to comfort me. The nuns were a teaching order but I never thought of myself teaching. I would contemplate the Five Glorious and the Five Sorrowful Mysteries.

I could hardly wait for the whole thing to be settled and approved. My father, I was sure, would be sympathetic. But when I thought of my mother's probable reaction, I hesitated, and decided to wait and argue the point when I was a little older.

When they came back from their journey to England I no longer boarded at the convent and the routine of church going to the Anglican church started again. After several Sundays, I began to waver. One of Mr. Dance's sermons made a great impression on me. The text was 'Faith without works is dead.' I couldn't help feeling there was a great deal of truth in it. Better perhaps to do good than to weep over the death of Jesus, or spend time longing to have lived then. Anyhow, I started looking round for good works. The trouble was that there didn't seem to be any.

My first good work was to help Victoria, our housemaid, with the washing up. But she looked at me suspiciously. 'What's this trap now?' her eyes said. She washed up very elaborately with two basins, and at last she grew tolerant enough to let me fish the plates out of the rinsing water and dry them. She never thanked me nor smiled at me, though she seemed to grow accustomed to my turning up. However, I soon got weary of her indifference. She didn't even sing her usual hymns when I was there.

Then I tried going to see an old coloured lady who lived near us. She was bedridden and I thought I'd read to her. Before I left her I always remembered to put a fan within her reach, her spectacles and a glass of water or milk, if any, for milk was scarce in Dominica. Her very small house looked onto the street and she always kept the door open so that she could chat with passers-by. I soon realised that she liked chatting far more than listening to me and also that if I hadn't been there one of her friends would certainly have come in to have a gossip with her. This obviously cheered her up far better than I could. So I gave that up.

I never said a word of my religious longings. But they knew, or guessed. I overheard my father saying, 'Don't tease her, she'll grow out of it.' So I wasn't teased. But I thought, 'Grow out of it? I'll never grow out of it. Never!' Sometimes, though, I saw in the way my mother looked at me that she longed to see the last of this particular phase of my growing up. During my religious fit she withdrew, not discouraging me, not arguing about something she thought quite excessive. However, I was too happy to care much about that. I don't think I've ever been quite so happy since.

Soon came the time during the hot weather when we went up to a small estate in the hills. After the sale of Bona Vista my father kept the smaller place, which I will call Morgan's Rest. It was hot, only about four hundred feet above sea level, if that. Not a beautiful place, just a pretty place. It was shut in behind two low hills which sloped down to the sea.

It was there, not in wild beautiful Bona Vista, that I began to feel I loved the land and to know that I would never forget it. There I would go for long walks alone. It's strange growing up in a very beautiful place and seeing that it is beautiful. It was alive, I was sure of it. Behind the bright colours the softness, the hills like clouds and the clouds like fantastic hills. There was something austere, sad, lost, all these things. I wanted to identify myself with it, to lose myself in it. (But it turned its head away, indifferent, and that broke my heart.)

The earth was like a magnet which pulled me and sometimes I came near it, this identification or annihilation that I longed for. Once, regardless of the ants, I lay down and kissed the earth and thought, 'Mine, mine.' I wanted to defend it from strangers. Why was I sure that in the end they would be defeated? They can't cut down the silent mountains or scoop up the eternal sea but they can do a lot. The trees and flowers they destroy will grow again and they will be forgotten.

I was aware of the existence of death, of misfortune, poverty, disease. I finally arrived at the certainty that the Devil was quite as powerful as God, perhaps more so. An unconscious Manichee. I didn't believe, as I read, that it was two faces of the same thing. It was a fight between the two and the Devil was responsible for everything that had gone wrong. I was passionately on the side of God, but it was very difficult to see what I could do about it.

There was a hammock on the verandah at Morgan's Rest. In the evening, swinging, I would watch the sunset and wonder why some people were so stupid as not to believe in God. I'd take no notice of the shouts of 'Stop that, the ropes are creaking!' The sadness which swooped and took possession so suddenly after sunset. Big, beautiful moths, flying beetles, swarming towards the lights. 'Night with its thousand eyes.' These Edwardian songs, how they cling.

> Night has a thousand eyes,
> Day but one.

Then it would be dark and although the stars and the fireflies would come out, I was glad to go inside to the light and to hear people's voices. The vase of roses (for my mother had green fingers and there was a bed of La France and Maréchal Neil roses she planted which soon flowered). The comforting shape of the old piano and on the music rack Braga's 'Serenata.' On the top, the score of *Flora Dora*, an American musical comedy.

> Tell me pretty maiden
> Are there any more at home like you?
> There are a few, kind sir,
> But simple girls and proper too.
> Tell me pretty maiden,
> What these very simple girlies do?

Their manners are perfection
And the opposite of mine.

Whenever I looked at Braga's 'Serenata' I felt rather uncomfortable because this had happened: The time came when I was allowed to come downstairs and join in the musical evenings to play the Welsh airs my father was so fond of. 'Gwenllian's Repose' was his favourite —'Don't keep the loud pedal down all the time for that one.' On this particular evening a certain Mr. Gregg had been persuaded to play his violin. He wanted to play Braga's 'Serenata' and I very confidently said that of course I could accompany him on the piano if he had the music. We started off and for one page all went well. Then I turned it and immediately we were playing different music.

'Something's wrong,' said Mr. Gregg. 'We'd better start again.'

We started again but as soon as the page was turned the same thing happened.

'You're playing wrong,' said Mr. Gregg, looking flustered.

'I'm playing what's written,' I said.

Mr. Gregg looked at my music. 'Yes, but haven't you forgotten the D.C. sign?' he said.

I looked and there it was, the da capo sign, and I hadn't noticed it.

'I'm so sorry,' I said and someone called, 'Third time lucky.' But Mr. Gregg, with a withering look at me, put his violin away and refused to play again.

He soon left and it was explained to me that he was a very lonely man who hardly ever played in public, but he'd been persuaded to just this once and I'd spoilt it, of course. So I could never look at Braga's 'Serenata' without feeling uncomfortable. I knew that for the rest of his life, whenever he thought of me, Mr. Gregg would send out a small shoot of dislike.

Morgan's Rest, though small, was very fertile. Cocoa was grown there as well as coffee, also nutmegs, and though my father could seldom be there himself, he had installed an overseer whose name was John.

It was Victoria, who came with us to the country, who told me that he was very anxious to learn to read and write. This seemed to me a marvellous opportunity to do good. His little house was not far from ours and I went to see him. He particularly wanted to learn to sign his name so that other people would never know how ignorant he was. I liked him very much. With my mother's consent we fixed it up and armed with a copy of *Reading Without Tears* I would go along to his house. I soon realised that teaching him was very different from teaching a child, for he had a man's mind and grasped everything very quickly. We got on like a house on fire and I looked forward to the lessons.

I think it was the fifth or sixth time I went there that we were interrupted by someone laughing very loudly in the doorway. I looked up and there was John's wife, just come in from work on the estate. She was a very big woman, much bigger than John himself. Her skirts were girded up far above her knees and she had a cutlass in her hand. The sharp edge looked blue. She didn't greet me or say anything, she just laughed but her eyes were not laughing. John took no notice of her; he didn't even look up. But I became more and more nervous.

At last I said that I had to be getting home as it was late, and as I was walking away I could hear her laughing: 'kyah, kyah, kyah.' I said nothing of this to my mother, but someone else must have told her, Victoria probably, for she said next day, 'John's wife doesn't like you going to their house, does she?'

'Well, no, I don't think she does much, but perhaps she'll get used to me,' I said.

My mother said I'd better not go there again. 'I believe she's rather a quarrelsome woman.'

I said that I had promised to teach him to sign his name. Couldn't I go back there just once more? She said yes, if I'd promised I must go, but that I must tell him I wouldn't come again.

His wife wasn't there when I went back and John said nothing, though he seemed a bit serious. Before I left he could sign his name in a round, clear hand and when I told him that this would be the last lesson he looked very reproachfully at me. It's not fair, I thought, he must know perfectly well that it is his wife's fault.

I felt sad walking back to my house. It would all get twisted, as everything gets twisted in the West Indies. Also I couldn't help feeling cheated that my guardian angel, whom I still half believed in, had let me down. I didn't want him to strike the woman dead exactly, but still he might have managed something.

Soon after this a man called Émile, who worked on the estate

and was a friend of John's, came to the door and said he wanted
to see my mother in private. She looked rather astonished and
took him into her room where they talked. At the end of the conversation Émile emerged with a rather stolid expression and as
soon as he had gone my mother sat down and laughed so heartily
that it was some time before she could tell us why she was laughing.

It turned out that Émile had asked for my hand in marriage and
promised her, if she would consent, a present of a large yam. I never
heard the last of that yam. 'You're only worth a yam,' they would say,
shrieking with mirth.

My mother said, 'Well, you insisted on going to John's house
against my advice.'

I couldn't help thinking again that all this was extremely unfair. I
had tried to do something I thought was worthy and it had ended with
my being ridiculed. I think this was the beginning of the end of my
religious fit. I began to doubt not only my guardian angel, but everything and everybody else. We went back to Roseau.

Then our fox terrier Rex, whom I was very fond of, got distemper.
He went blind, foamed at the mouth and none of the servants would
go near him. I knew that my father didn't think he would recover but
I implored him for time. I was praying and praying, and surely my
prayers would be answered. Perhaps people could be compensated
in heaven, but animals have no souls and don't go to heaven, so why?
Why? Rex was put out of his misery while I was asleep. After that I
decided that the Devil was undoubtedly stronger than God, so what
was the use?

My father, wanting to cheer me up, told me that I was old enough
to have a dress allowance. It was not a very large dress allowance but
I began to feel grown up. I bought a red tam-o'-shanter. I tried to
learn to play tennis. I could seldom get the ball over the net but I
persevered.

God and the Devil were very far away. I used to pray once, kneeling
at the open window of my bedroom, looking at the stars, but now I
seldom prayed, or very mechanically. But I still knelt at the open
window, looking and wondering.

The Southern Cross, for example, had it been put there especially
to celebrate the death of Christ? I didn't know but I thought it

probably was. Sometimes the stars were close and benevolent, other nights, far, far away, quite indifferent.

Wondering what my life would be like now that God and the Devil were far away. And the sea, sometimes so calm and blue and beautiful but underneath the calm—what? Things like sharks and barracudas are bad enough but who knows, not the wisest fisherman nor the most experienced sailor, what lives in the Cuba deep.

Not think about it! I preferred to see it in the distance, the blue, the treacherous, tremendous sea.

The Zouaves

I CAN JUST REMEMBER the old Anglican church, small, cool and shadowy. When it was pulled down to make room for a larger building I couldn't imagine what my father meant when he said the new one was hideous. It was very bright and hot, with shiny pitch-pine pews and purple-red stained-glass windows. It was divided into two parts, one for the white people in front, the other for the black people at the back; there was a space between. There wasn't a large black congregation for they were nearly all Catholics on the Caribbean side of the island. But a certain number of devout black women came Sunday after Sunday, and a sprinkling of men. At the end of the service they went out of one door and we went out of another. I don't think anybody minded this or even noticed it. I certainly didn't. It had always been so, it would always be so, like the sun or the rain.

One Sunday, as we were waiting for the clergyman to emerge from the vestry followed by a procession of dark choirboys (for he was as High Church as he dared to be), I was startled to see two tall black men come in, walk up the aisle and sit down among the white people. Not only that, but they were shown into one of the front pews which happened to be empty. Not only that, but they were quite the most splendid people I had ever seen. They wore baggy red trousers caught at the ankle, short yellow jackets, white caps and white boots. I think the yellow jackets opened onto white shirts and there was a sash, but it was a long time ago and I can't be sure of the details. I recognised the Zouave uniform for I had seen photographs and pictures of it, but no photograph could give anything like the dazzling effect of the real thing. I kept my eyes on them all through the service. I didn't think it at all likely that they were decent, sober and respectable Anglicans. There were soldiers stationed in one of the other islands, perhaps in Castries, St. Lucia. I had heard vaguely that the West Indian regiment wore the Zouave uniform by special request of Queen Victoria. Perhaps they were visiting relatives in Roseau and wished to see our church out of curiosity.

After the service they came out with the rest of us and I saw them walk up the street talking and laughing. No one said anything about them as we walked home, but I puzzled about them for the rest of the day and the day after that. Like Queen Victoria I had fallen in love with the uniform. Dressed like that it would be impossible not to be brave, impossible not to be bold, reckless and all the things I admired so much.

We had at that time a very energetic administrator called Mr. Hesketh. That was part of his name anyway. The governor of the Leeward Islands—at this time we were Leeward and not Windward —lived in Antigua. So did the Chief Justice. So did the Anglican bishop. But Mr. Hesketh, our administrator, went his own active way and did what he liked. He improved the roads out of all knowledge and triumphantly carried through his better idea of an imperial road across the island so that the Caribbean and South Atlantic sides were no longer cut off one from the other. He got an English engineer for this and the work took a long time.

Meanwhile he arranged for a small coasting steamer called the *Yare* to carry passengers and goods from one end of the island to the other. He tried to tackle the sewage problem but here even he failed. However, he gave several prizes for the best-dressed mask at the yearly carnival and was a great patron of the local cricket club.

One day the rumour started that Mr. Hesketh was going to give a fancy-dress ball for his little niece, who was staying at Government House with her father and mother. The rumour was true, it was to be a fancy-dress dance for children, and the invitations were sent out.

Auntie B cut out dresses very well. She didn't live with us but she would often pay us a visit and it was decided that she would make my dress for the ball. When my mother asked me what I would like to go as, I answered at once that I should like to be a Zouave for the evening. My aunt asked me ironically if I really thought she was capable of making a Zouave uniform. I then said I wanted to be a gypsy. They reminded me that the gypsy colours, red and yellow, would not suit me as I was too fair. As I couldn't go as a Zouave and couldn't go as a gypsy, I lost interest in the whole thing. My mother subscribed to a magazine from London which was called the *Glass of Fashion Up-to-Date.* In one of the back numbers was a long illustrated article suggesting fancy dresses for children. I watched her very indifferently as she turned the pages and when at length they decided I should go as 'yachting,' I agreed. But dressed to go to the dance, I stared at myself in the glass with rising happiness and excitement, for I was transformed. I had always imagined that my aunt didn't like me much, but the colour she had chosen was exactly right, a blue-green which reminded you of the sea, and my eyes were no longer pale but reflected the colour. The dress had a tight bodice and ankle-length full skirt. The nuns had also become excited at the idea of having a fancy-dress ball and had presented me with a net flounce. This was ornamented with cut-out paper fish, golden red, and was tacked onto the hem of the dress, which was otherwise quite plain.

As soon as I got to Government House several people congratulated me on my dress. And Mr. Hesketh came up and asked me to dance the first waltz with him. Among his other accomplishments he was a very good dancer indeed and like all good dancers he could make his partner feel she too was an expert.

All the furniture had been taken out of the room, there was only the dark polished slippery floor with a few chairs set round it, the white walls and the music. I don't remember whether it was the local band, which consisted of a concertina, a steel triangle and what they call a shakshak, or perhaps it was a piano and violin. In any case the musicians were behind a screen. I longed for that waltz to last forever, to skim forever round and round with Mr. Hesketh's arm about me. I stopped being shy and managed to laugh and talk to him. I waltzed three times with Mr. Hesketh and each time was better than the last and I was happier. I went home, I suppose, somewhere between twelve and one and looking at myself in the glass I knew that that night had changed me. I was a different girl, I told myself that I would be just as happy the next day, now I would always be happy.

In the afternoons when I came home from school I often went for
a ride. If I was with friends we could go wherever we liked, to the lake,
the waterfall, anywhere. But if I was by myself I was supposed to go
over the bridge and along the flat, safe road between Canefields and
Goodwill estates. The sugar cane hadn't been cut, there was a green
sea on one side and a blue sea on the other. Dominica horses never
trotted. They walked, ambled, cantered and sometimes could be
persuaded to gallop. So I was ambling along when I saw in the
distance Mr. Hesketh driving a small trap.

The moment I saw him I became very nervous. He was driving
towards Roseau, I was riding away from it. We must inevitably meet.
He seemed to be coming along very fast, I had no time to think what
I should say, to prepare myself for the meeting as it were. Almost at
once we seemed to be side by side. He took his hat off, waved it at
me and called something. Overcome with shyness I turned my head
away and pretended not to see him. Then he was gone and I rode on,
knowing that I had behaved in a foolish, bad-mannered way. I tried
to console myself by saying that no one had seen us, no one would
ever know.

It was some days afterwards that my mother said to me, 'Why were
you so rude to Mr. Hesketh?' I stared at her and said, 'Do you mean
that he told you?' 'Oh, he made a joke about it,' said my mother.
'While we were playing croquet he asked me what he had done to
offend you. He said that you met him on the Goodwill road and cut
him dead. He was laughing.'

I could only say that I didn't mean to be rude. 'You are a very
peculiar child,' said my mother. 'There are times when I am very
anxious about you. I can't imagine what will happen if you don't learn
to behave more like other people.'

I didn't answer this; I only told myself that never again would I like
Mr. Hesketh or think about him. I was also very miserable.

Leaving Dominica

THIS IS THE LAST CONVERSATION I can remember with my father. Though I cannot of course put it down word for word, I can remember the gist of it. He called me into his consulting room and told me to sit on the sofa. The first thing he asked me was whether I liked my Aunt Clarice, and I answered cautiously that I wasn't sure she liked me very much. He said, 'Clarice doesn't wear her heart on her sleeve. You have to get to know her.' I said, 'But I'll be going to England.' 'Yes,' he said, 'that's just the trouble, you'll be going to England.' Then he said briskly, 'Of course it's going to be very different, but you'll have to get used to that.' Then: 'If you're very unhappy, or want anything very much, you must write directly to me. But don't write at the first shock or I'll be disappointed in you.' I said, 'Yes,' and he said he would be going up to the club and would be late for dinner, and would I tell my mother.

He came with my aunt and myself as far as Bridgetown, Barbados, where we caught the ocean boat. When we said goodbye he hugged me tightly but I said, 'Goodbye, goodbye,' very cheerfully, for already I was on my way to England. Down in the cabin which I shared with my aunt I saw that the little coral brooch which I was wearing had been crushed. I had been very fond of it; now I took it off and put it away without any particular feeling. Already all my childhood, the West Indies, my father and mother had been left behind; I was forgetting them. They were the past.

IT BEGAN TO
GROW COLD

The material which follows was not
considered by Jean Rhys to be finished
work. Some of it is little more than notes.

First Steps

ON THE SEA it was still warm at first and I loved it, although I could not get over the huge amount that people ate. First there was a large breakfast, all sorts of unfamiliar dishes. At eleven o'clock the steward came round with cups of Bovril. Then a huge lunch of four or five courses.

I ate my way steadily through and could scarcely walk when I got up. Then my aunt explained that we were meant to take only a little of each course. Lunch wasn't over until half past two. At five, tea: another huge meal with cakes, bread and butter, jam. Dinner at eight o'clock was the most important meal and the longest. The orchestra playing at meals enchanted me. They gave a concert and I sang. Everyone applauded and I told my aunt that when I got to London I would go straight onto the stage. She laughed heartily.

Then, quite suddenly it seemed, it began to grow cold. The sky was grey, not blue. The sea was sometimes rough. My aunt sat on deck in a thick coat with rugs round her. There were rugs for me too, but still I shivered. It was a very grey day when we reached Southampton and when I looked out of the porthole my heart sank. Then I thought, 'Now at last I shall see a train.' I had seen toy trains. They were always brightly coloured, green, red, blue, so I stood on a platform at Southampton station bewildered because I could see nothing that resembled a train.

'But I don't see the train, where is it?'

'Right in front of you,' said my aunt and stepped into what I thought was a brown, dingy little room. There were racks overhead and people sitting in the corners. This, then, was a train. I said nothing and after a while the train started.

Before long we were plunged into black darkness. A railway accident, I thought. We came into the light again. 'Was that a railway accident?' 'No, it was a tunnel,' my aunt said, laughing.

We stayed at a boardinghouse somewhere in Bloomsbury; it may have been Upper Bedford Place. The first morning I was in London I woke up very early. I lay for what seemed an age. There wasn't a sound but I wanted to see what London looked like so I got up, put on my clothes and went out. The street door must have been bolted, not locked, or perhaps the key was in the door. At any rate I got out quite easily into a long, grey, straight street. It was misty but not cold. There were not many people about, nor much traffic. I think I must have found my way into New Oxford Street and then walked to Holborn. It was all the same, long, straight, grey, a bit disappointing. I began to feel hungry, and as I had kept careful count of the turnings I was soon on my way back. It must have been about half past seven. When I tried the door it was open and there was a maid in the passage who seemed astonished when she saw me. I said 'Good morning' but she didn't answer.

On my way to my room I passed the bathroom and thought it would be a good idea to have a bath. I felt not hot, but sticky and a little tired. So I went in and turned the hot water tap on. When the bath was half full I undressed and got in, thinking it very pleasant. I began to feel rather happy and thought that when the water got cool I would turn the hot tap on again. I began to sing. Then above the noise of the water came a loud voice.

'Who's that in there?'

I answered with my name.

'Turn that tap off,' said the voice. 'Turn that tap off at once.'

I turned it off. All my pleasure had gone and I got out of the bath and into my clothes as quickly as I could. When I reached my room my aunt was waiting for me. I said, 'I'm afraid the landlady is very annoyed with me.'

'Of course she's annoyed with you,' said my aunt. 'What possessed you to go into the bathroom and take all the hot water?'

'I didn't mean to take all the hot water,' I said. 'I just wanted to have a bath. After all, it's a fairly natural thing to have in the morning.'

My aunt said, 'It didn't occur to you that nobody else would have any hot water at all?'

'I never thought of that,' I said.

'I've already noticed,' said my aunt, 'that you are quite incapable of thinking about anyone else but yourself.'

I didn't answer this though there were many things I wanted to say: that English plumbing was a mystery to me, that indoor lavatories shocked me, that I thought a tap marked 'H' would automatically spout hot water, that it never occurred to me that the supply was limited and where did it come from anyway?

My aunt then explained the ritual of having a bath in an English boardinghouse. You had to ask for it several days beforehand, you had to be very careful to take it at that time and no other, and so on and so on.

All through breakfast the landlady glared at me. My aunt wouldn't speak to me. I could hardly swallow my eggs and bacon. 'We are going to see the Wallace Collection this morning,' said my aunt. 'Are you ready?'

For the next few days my aunt showed me the sights: Westminster Abbey, St. Paul's, the zoo. I don't know what reaction she expected but I know that I disappointed her. For instance, I liked the outside of Westminster Abbey but when we went in I thought it a muddle, a jumble of statues and memorial tablets. Hardly room to move, I thought. 'Don't you think it's wonderful?' she said. 'Yes, but rather crowded.' I thought St. Paul's too cold, too Protestant. I looked for one bit of warmth and colour but couldn't find it. In the Wallace Collection I fell asleep when she left me on a bench.

As for the zoo, I simply hated it. We saw the lions first and I thought the majestic lion looked at me with such sad eyes, pacing, pacing up and down, never stopping. Then we made a special journey to see the Dominica parrot. The grey bird was hunched in on himself, the most surly, resentful parrot I had ever seen. I said 'Hello' to him but he wouldn't even look at me. 'Of course, he is very old,' said my aunt. 'Nobody knows how old.'

'Poor bird,' I said.

Then the alligators and crocodiles, which frightened me so much

I could barely look at them. Then the snakes. Finally we went to see the hummingbirds. The hummingbirds finished me.

I believe that it is quite different now, but then they were in a little side room, the floor very dirty. Thick slices of bread smeared with marmalade or jam of some sort were suspended on wires. The birds were flying around in a bewildered way. Trying desperately to get out, it seemed to me. Even their colours were dim. I got such an impression of hopeless misery that I couldn't bear to look. My aunt finally asked me if I had enjoyed it and I said yes I had, but then and there I decided that nothing would ever persuade me to go into a zoo again.

The first time I felt a sense of wonder in England was when we, a few of the boarders at the Perse School for Girls, Cambridge, were taken to Ely Cathedral. There were no pews or chairs, only a space, empty, and the altar, and stained-glass windows. The pillars on either side were like a stone forest. I was so excited and moved that I began to tremble.

The classical mistress, Miss Patey, was in charge of the flock. Afterwards we went to have tea with one of her friends. We sat on a verandah with flagstones. I took the cup of tea that was offered to me but my hands were shaking so much that I dropped the cup, which was, of course, smashed. I mumbled some sort of apology and just for a moment the hostess looked at the pieces with a regretful face. Miss Patey apologised.

I left the Perse School after one term. I had written to my father about my great wish to be an actress, and true to his promise he wrote back, 'That is what you must do.'

The Royal Academy of Dramatic Art, then known colloquially as Tree's School after the manager of His Majesty's Theatre, hadn't been going very long when I went there. Otherwise I doubt whether I would have had the chance to go. I was surprised when I found I had passed the so-called entrance examination. My aunt, who disapproved of the whole affair, left me in a boardinghouse in Upper Bedford Place, very excited and anxious to do my best. I was seventeen.

The Academy was divided into the A's, the B's and the C's. The A's were the new students, the B's were half way, and I never met any of the C's. Well-known actors and actresses would arrive to advise the C's, but we never saw them except in passing. When matinée idols like Henry Ainley arrived, the girls would haunt the passages hoping to catch a glimpse of them, but they would pass along quickly, and also one wasn't supposed to look.

The A's were taught by an actress whose Christian name was Gertrude. I have forgotten her surname. The B's we sometimes met in a room downstairs presided over by a woman called Hetty. Here you could get coffee and sandwiches and here I met several of the B's and came to dislike them. I thought them conceited and unkind. Once, when I left my furs behind and came back to fetch them, I heard someone say, 'Is this goat or monkey?'

I must confess that my furs, like all my clothes, were hideous, for my aunt's one idea had been to fit me out as cheaply as possible. When we bought my one dress, my everyday wear, the skirt was far too long even for those days but she said to have it altered would be too expensive, I could tuck it up at the waist and because I was so thin nobody would notice. So apparelled, I set off to be inspected by the A's, the B's and the C's.

Miss Gertrude was quite a good teacher, I think. One of our first lessons was to learn how to laugh. This was comparatively easy. You sang the do re mi fa sol la ti do, and done quickly enough it did turn out to be a laugh, though rather artificial. Our next lesson was to learn how to cry. 'And now, watch me,' said Miss Gertrude. She turned away for a few seconds, and when she turned back tears were coursing down her face, which itself remained unmoved. 'Now try,' she said. The students stood in a row trying to cry. 'Think of something sad,' whispered the girl next to me. I looked along the line and they were all making such hideous faces in their attempts to cry that I began to laugh. Miss Gertrude never approved of me.

We had lessons in fencing, dancing, gesture (Delsarte) and elocution. In the elocution master's class there was once a scene which puzzled me and made me feel sad. It upset me because the master, whose name was Mr. Heath, was the only one except for the gesture woman who gave me the slightest encouragement or took any notice of me, and Honour, the pupil who quarrelled with him, was the only one I really liked. We had even been to a matinée together, accompanied by a sour-faced maid. We were reciting a poem in which the word 'froth' occurred, and Honour refused to pronounce the word as Mr. Heath did. 'Froth,' said the elocution master. 'Frawth,' said the pupil. For a long time they shouted at each other: 'Froth'—'Frawth' —'Froth'—'Frawth.' I listened to this appalled. 'Froth'—'Frawth'— 'Froth'—'Frawth.' At last Honour said: 'I refuse to pronounce the word "froth." "Froth" is cockney and I'm not here to learn cockney.' Her face was quite white, with the freckles showing. 'I think you mean to be rude,' Mr. Heath said. 'Will you leave the class, please.' Honour stalked out, white as a sheet. 'We will now go on with the lesson,' said Mr. Heath, red as a beet. There was no end to the scandal. Honour was taken away from the school by her mother, who had written a book on the proper pronunciation of English. Mr. Heath either was dismissed or left. This gave me my first insight into the snobbishness and unkindness that went on.

Part of our training was that every week some of us would have to act a well-known scene before Miss Gertrude, and she would criticise it and say who was right and who was wrong. We usually played a scene from *Lady Windermere's Fan* or *Paulo and Francesca* by Stephen Philips. I soon got caught up with five or six other students.

A man we called Toppy was a bit of a clown and announced that he intended to go into music hall, not the straight theatre. The other man of our group, to my great surprise, asked me to marry him. Having a proposal made me feel as if I had passed an examination. He wrote me a long letter which started by saying he noticed that my landlady bullied me and that I had better get away from her by marrying him. He then talked about money. He said that as he was now twenty-one he had come into his money, and he was anxious to meet my aunt to explain matters to her. He ended the letter by saying that if I would consent we would spend our honeymoon in Africa, travelling from the Cape to Cairo. The trip did sound tempting, but I answered the letter solemnly that my only wish was to be a great actress. After some thought I crossed out *great* and put *good.* When we met afterwards at the Academy he didn't seem at all embarrassed, and never referred to either his letter or my answer.

One of the girls with whom for a time I made friends was half Turkish. She asked me to tea at her rooms and spent all the time talking about a hectic love affair. 'You don't know anything about it,' she'd say, then proceed to tell me all about it at great length. One

day when I went there she was darning some stockings. She said, 'I
expect you are very surprised to see someone like me darning stockings.' I said, 'No, why?' From that time on our friendship cooled. She
stopped inviting me to tea.

At that time there was a dancer called Maud Allen playing at the
Palace Theatre. She was a barefoot dancer as they called it then, and
wore vaguely classic Greek clothes. She was, of course, imitating
Isadora Duncan. A lot of people in London were shocked by her and
when in one of her dances she brought in the head of John the Baptist
on a dish, there was quite a row and she had to cut that bit out. One
day our dancing teacher said, 'Maud Allen is *not* a dancer. She doesn't
even begin to be a dancer. But if I told her to run across the stage
and pretend to pick a flower she would do it, and do it well. I'm afraid
I cannot say the same of all the young ladies in this class, and I advise
you all to go to the Palace and watch Maud Allen. It might do you
a lot of good.'

During vacation from the Academy I went to Harrogate to visit an
uncle. It was there that I heard of my father's death. My mother wrote
that she could not afford to keep me at the Academy and that I must
return to Dominica. I was determined not to do that, and in any case
I was sure that they didn't want me back. My aunt and I met in
London to buy hot-climate clothes, and when she was doing her own
shopping I went to a theatrical agent in the Strand, called Blackmore,
and got a job in the chorus of a musical comedy called *Our Miss Gibbs.*

Chorus Girls

I WAS A YEAR and a half to two years in *Our Miss Gibbs*. In the winter we toured small towns in the north, and in the summer the seaside places. The chorus girls' wages were thirty-five shillings a week and extra for every matinée. When you signed the contract you gave them the option for the next tour so long as it was work you were capable of doing. It was a steady job. There was, however, a dreadful gap after the winter tour finished and before the summer tour started. It was impossible to save enough to tide you over this gap, so most of the girls lived at home for those two or three months. The few who, like myself, had no home tried to get a job in what were known as music hall sketches, which went on all the year round.

In one of the gaps I managed to be taken on in the chorus of a music hall sketch called *Chanticleer*. The name was taken from a Paris revue that was a great success at that time. Ours was an appalling show. The biggest joke in it was a girl in tights walking across the stage, dropping an egg and clucking loudly. Only one or two of the girls were at all attractive and we were hardly rehearsed. However, we opened at a town in the north and there we were, waiting in the wings, ready to go on. It was cold and I was shivering. We heard a loud tramping noise and somebody said, 'What on earth's that?' The answer was: 'That's the gallery walking out.' The gallery didn't hiss or boo if they disliked a show, they simply walked out, making as much noise as possible. When it was our turn to go on with our very amateurish dance I was shivering with fear as well as with cold.

As soon as we began I felt the mockery and scorn coming up from the audience like smoke. I was at the end of the line, near the wings, and after a bit of this I simply left the line and went offstage. Before I left I looked at the girl next to me. Her face was grim. She felt it as much as I did but bravely she went on dancing. I took my make-up off and went back to my lodgings feeling very unhappy at being so cowardly. I kept thinking, 'She stuck it, why couldn't I?' I made up my mind that on the next night I would stick it whatever they did, whether they hissed, booed or even threw things.

I was in the dressing room with the other girls, making up, when the callboy knocked and said, 'Will Miss Gray please go to Mr. Peterman's office at once.' Gray was the name I was using then. Mr. Peterman was the owner and manager of the show. As soon as I got into the room I saw he was in a towering rage. As he glared at me with a tight mouth he looked terrifying. 'Why,' he said, 'did you walk offstage in the middle of the act last night? Were you ill?'

'No, I wasn't ill,' I said. 'I was frightened.'

'And what were you frightened of?'

I said that I was frightened of the audience.

He said, 'And what the hell are you doing on the stage, may I ask, if you are frightened of an audience? You can take off your make-up and go home. I don't want to have anything more to do with you, letting down the show like that.'

I said, 'Well, I shouldn't have run away, I know, but I think you ought to give me my fare back to London.'

'And why should I give you your fare? I'll do nothing of the sort.'

I had no money at all, so—as always when I am desperate—I was able to fight.

There was a society called, I think, 'for the Protection of Chorus Girls.' I knew the address and I said, 'Mr. Peterman, if you don't give me my fare back to London I will write to the society and complain about you.' He growled. I had never before heard a man growl like a dog, but he did. He said, 'There's an excursion train to London tomorrow. I'll give you the money for that, nothing else.'

When I returned to the dressing room to take my make-up off, the girl next to me said, 'Peterman's in an awful rage because I think he's got hardly any bookings for this show.'

'I don't wonder,' I said.

I was used to sleeping late and the excursion train left at some abnormally early hour. I was so afraid of missing it that I sat up all night, suitcase at my feet, waiting. When I got to London and to my aunt, who was there at the time, she said, 'Whatever have you been doing with yourself? You look shocking. You'd better go and have a bath at once, you're so dirty.'

I have forgotten how I got over the rest of the gap. I suppose my aunt helped me. Later I went back to *Our Miss Gibbs*.

There was an elaborate dancer in the show, what they called a speciality dancer, and the speciality dancer and the chorus girls were at daggers drawn. She would seldom have anything to do with us; the chorus, in retaliation, responded by attacking her appearance, her manners, her morals. Every possible vice was piled on the poor girl. She had a little dog with her, and the sort of thing the chorus girls said was that she kept the dog to make love to her. I used to watch her from the wings because I loved her dance, and I didn't think she was bad, though rather haughty and touch-me-not. I knew the things said about her were unfair.

People talk about chorus girls as if they were all exactly alike, all immoral, all silly, all on the make. As a matter of fact, far from being all alike they were rather a strange mixture. One of them was the daughter of a well-known Labour leader and we noticed that whenever a Conservative victory had been won and we all cheered (for we were all Conservatives), she cheered more than any of us. We decided she hated her father. Another girl was the daughter of a woman who stood up for Oscar Wilde. There were chorus girls of sixteen and chorus girls of nearly forty; the contract signed with George Dance for *Our Miss Gibbs* enabled you to stay forever if you liked, until you were old and grey. Besides, the older ones often had good voices and were very useful. Some, though not many, were married. Some were engaged to be married and looking forward to their marriages like any other girl. Some were very ambitious, determined to make a good marriage (which was quite possible), and if you imagine they ever did anything which might interfere with that you don't know the type. Some were ambitious to get on in the theatre. These were rather

The church at Gyffylliog in Denbighshire where Jean Rhys's paternal grand-father, William Rees Williams, died in 1900 after being rector of the parish for twenty-six years.

'Willie and Minna's first house, *Stowe*. "Love in a Cottage," February 15th, 1866.' It was probably Jean Rhys's 'Auntie B' who painted this watercolour.

Dr. Rees Williams's house in Roseau, Dominica, photographed in 1970. The gallery has been enclosed to form rooms and the large garden in which the house once stood has vanished.

The twin sisters
Minna Rees Williams,
Jean Rhys's mother (right),
and Brenda Lockhart—
'Auntie B' (below).

Jean Rhys is the girl on the extreme right in this photograph.

Our only photograph of Jean Rhys (left) in Paris. It is almost certain that her companion is Germaine Richelot.

Jean Lenglet sent Jean Rhys this picture of himself and their daughter after they had separated.

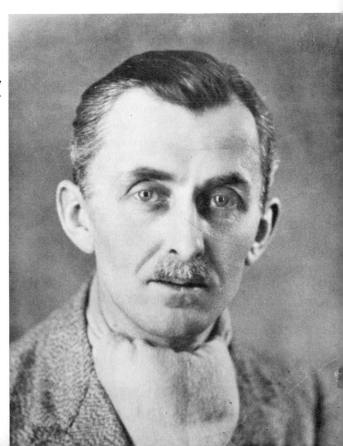

Leslie Tilden Smith, Jean Rhys's second husband.

Jean Rhys in Dominica
during the thirties, the only
time she revisited the island.

All that was left of the Geneva garden when she revisited it.

The last photograph taken of Jean Rhys, several weeks before her death.

few and far between and I noticed that nearly all of them came from theatrical families.

There was always the company tart, but no one ever called her a tart. They just said, 'So-and-so has a lot of friends.' She would seldom turn up for the train calls, for someone would be sure to take her by car from one town to the next. I will never forget the face of the stage manager when a girl called Nancy was missing for the rehearsal call on a Monday. A telegram was brought in to him, he opened it and said in a bewildered voice, '*Contretemps*—what the devil does she mean, *contretemps?*' I think it was a day or two before Nancy turned up, and somebody else had to be taught her dance.

We travelled with theatrical baskets which were collected by the theatrical baggage man every Thursday and went with the scenery. So we were left with small suitcases with washing things, toothbrush and very minimal make-up. Sunday was travelling day. The classic joke about travelling was two railway men talking. 'What have you got there, Bill?' 'Fish and actors.' 'Oh, shove them on a siding.'

Everybody knew the good theatrical lodgings, and everyone knew they were taken in advance. We had to do the best we could. Sometimes we struck lucky, sometimes not. You could save a bit if you lived with another girl, more if you lived with two. The food was always the same. We would get to the new lodgings after our Sunday train journey to a large joint of beef, usually very tough. On Monday we had it warmed up. On Tuesday minced. On Wednesday shepherd's pie or stew. On Thursday something exotic like eggs and bacon or liver. On Friday it was go as you can. On Saturday we were much too busy packing. On Sunday we left for another town which was exactly like the last one, or so I thought. All this was in the winter, in the north.

I never liked our landladies, but one I hated. I was living with a girl called Billie, and we were waiting upstairs with our suitcases packed when the landlady came in and presented us with her bill. It was enormous, about three times what we were expecting. Billie gave one look at it and said, 'We're not going to pay this!' The landlady said, 'Oh, yes you will, or you won't leave here.' She left the room and locked the door. Billie and I emptied our purses and there wasn't nearly enough to pay her, nor to pay the fare to the next town if we missed our train. Billie said, 'There's only one thing to do about this,' and opened the window. We were on the second floor but the snow was very thick on the ground down below. Billie said, 'Well, here's to it.' She threw her suitcase out and jumped after it. She lay still on the ground and I was frightened. After a while she looked up and said, 'Come on.' I wondered if it was awful but I didn't ask her. I threw my suitcase out too, and jumped. It was an awful bump in spite of the snow and for a while I lay still, wondering if I was dead. Then Billie said, 'Come on,' so I got up, and we were running out of the garden gate with our suitcases when we saw the landlady looking after us and frowning. Billie said, 'One word to you!' and together we ran out of the gate, laughing. From this time dated my irrevocable hatred of landladies.

In England my love and longing for books completely left me. I never felt the least desire to read anything, not even a newspaper, and I think this indifference lasted a long time. Years. I don't remember reading anything on tour except *Forest Lovers*. *Forest Lovers* was a book set in the Middle Ages, about a man and a girl who loved each other very much and who escaped into the forest to hide, but they always slept with a sword between them. All the girls in the dressing room had read the book and the conversation about the sword was endless. 'What did they have to do that for? Why? Besides, you could easily get over the sword.' 'No you couldn't, you'd get cut.' 'Of course you wouldn't.' The company tart, whom I liked very much, would sometimes lend me a book. I wouldn't really read it and sometimes I'd forget it, and she would embarrass me at train calls by shouting down the platform: 'Now then, Verney, what've you done with my book?' However abominable and dull my life was, it never occurred to me to buy a book or even a newspaper, which now seems very strange to me.

Going from room to room in this cold dark country, England, I never knew what it was that spurred me on and gave me an absolute certainty that there would be something else for me before long. Now I think the 'something else' was something small and limited. I realize that I was no good on the stage, forgot my lines, didn't thirst for the theatre as some of the girls did, yet I was so sure.

I got sick of being in *Our Miss Gibbs,* sick of wearing old Gaiety dresses cleaned. So we left—who was the girl I left with? I have

forgotten—and got a job in the chorus of a pantomime at the Old
Lyceum Theatre. The Tiller girls used to dance in it. I remember the
song they sang:

> Away down
> In jungle town
> Honeymoon
> Is coming soon
> And we hear the serenade
> To a pretty monkey maid
> And now in jungle town
> The moon shines down
> Without a frown
> I'll be true
> To monkey doodle-doo.

Then the Tiller girls danced, their heels clacking.

> I'll be true
> To monkey doodle-doo.

There were supposed to be rats in the dressing room but I never
saw one. By now my first real affair with a man had started. The
pantomime didn't run for long and I didn't try for anything afterwards. I knew that however crudely Mr. Peterman had spoken when
he asked what the hell I was doing on the stage, he had spoken the
truth, but my lover imagined that I could get on in the theatre and
insisted that I should have singing and dancing lessons. Dutifully I
attended them. The rest of the time I spent looking out of the window
for the messenger boy, because he always sent his letters by messenger.

The Interval

WHEN MY FIRST love affair came to an end I wrote this poem:

> I didn't know
> I didn't know
> I didn't know.

Then I settled down to be miserable.

But it still annoys me when my first object of worship is supposed to be a villain. Or perhaps the real idea at the back of this is that his class was oppressing mine. He had money. I had none.

On the contrary, I realise now what a very kind man he must have been. I was an ignorant girl, a shy girl. And when I read novels describing present-day love-making I realise I was also a passive, dull girl. Though I couldn't control my hammering heart when he touched me, I was too shy to say 'I love you.' It would be too much, too important. I couldn't claim so much.

When I first met this man I rather disliked him, and why I came to worship him I don't quite know. I loved his voice, the way he walked. He was like all the men in all the books I had ever read about London. He lived in Berkeley Square, and I got used to the warmth, the fires all over the house, the space, the comfort. When I left to go back to my rather cold room I was never envious. It was right, I felt. Sometimes the taxi drivers who took me home were nice, sometimes they weren't. One day he said to me, half laughing, 'Your taxi driver last

night came back and said you had vomited all over his cab and he
wanted quite a lot of compensation. Did you?' 'No, of course I didn't.'
He laughed and said, 'I thought you didn't.' This put me on his side
against the others, who were, I realised even at that time, vaguely
threatening his sort. He was a dream come true for me and one
doesn't question dreams, or envy them.

One day, lunching at what I suppose was the Savoy upstairs because we could see the Thames (I knew the ground-floor Grill
Room fairly well, from which you couldn't see the river), there
was another girl and another man with my lover and me, and they
started a long conversation about whether a certain actress really
washed her hair in Lux flakes. One would say, 'Yes she does, I
know her.' The other would say, 'I know her too, and she doesn't.
She only says she does for the money.' The argument about this
and kindred subjects went on and on, and I didn't know the actress and wasn't interested in whether or not she washed her hair
in Lux flakes, though my friend made every effort to drag me into
the conversation.

At the end of the meal, when the waiter had cleared and brought
the coffee, he dived under the table and came up with a very shabby
powder compact which, without expression, he put on the white
tablecloth. One of the first presents my lover had given me was a very
nice powder compact from Asprey's. It was difficult to open and I had
stuck to my old one because I was convinced that it brought me luck,
but on the white tablecloth it looked abominable. Most of the gilt had
worn off and the black underneath showed. Everyone looked at it
without speaking, with a sort of horror. I said in a sullen voice, 'It's
mine.' I grabbed it and put it in my handbag. How could I explain
to these strangers that I had used it all through my touring days as
a mascot?

Then they began talking about going to Hendon to see the flying.
I refused to go with them, partly because I wasn't in the least interested in aeroplanes and partly because I didn't want to see a new
thing with them. They went off and my lover took me to my room in
a taxi. I thought he would say at once, 'Why don't you use the new
compact I bought you at Asprey's?' Instead he said, 'Why didn't you
want to go on and see the flying?' I said, 'I don't want to see it with
them, or anything with them.' The taxi went on. Suddenly he put his

hand out and squeezed mine. I was very happy. I thought, 'I have not
only a lover, but a friend. How lucky I am.'

He said, 'Well, what do you propose to do with yourself this afternoon?' I said that I'd arranged with a friend to have tea, then go to
a music hall. This was untrue but I had already learnt that it was bad
policy to say that you were lonely or unhappy.

After he left me at my room I went for a long walk, trying to think
what it was that Nancy Erwin had that I hadn't. Nancy had ended with
a very elaborate marriage, a thing she was determined on from the
start. You saw her photographs in the *Sketch* and the *Tatler.* She didn't
have a shabby powder compact. She had a handkerchief with a powder puff in the middle so she could powder her face while pretending
she was just blowing her nose. Her handkerchief was always plaid,
and if it dropped and a waiter picked it up she would say, 'My little
bit of Scotch,' and everyone would laugh. What was the difference
between Nancy and me? It was that she was ruthless and I wasn't.

The next time I saw my lover he said he was going away to New
York on business.

Christmas Day

YEARS LATER, speaking to a Frenchman in Paris, I said, 'I can abstract myself from my body.' He looked so shocked that I asked if I was speaking bad French. He said, *'Oh non, mais . . . c'est horrible.'* And yet for so long that was what I did.

After what was then called an illegal operation, I stayed in a flat in Langham Street. I didn't suffer from remorse or guilt. I didn't think at all as women are supposed to think; my predominant feeling was one of intense relief, but I was very tired. I was not at all unhappy. It was like a pause in my life, a peaceful time. I didn't see him but he sent me a big rose plant in a pot and a very beautiful Persian kitten.

I saw his cousin Julian almost daily. I grew quite used to him and forgot that I hated him. It seemed natural that he should take charge of everything, supplying money, somehow producing a daily woman. He even took me out once, to a night club. One day he remarked that I was looking very peaky and told me I should go to the seaside for a week, and I agreed. I went to Ramsgate. I put the kitten in a home in Euston Road which had been recommended to me. I can't remember anything about Ramsgate but when I got back to London the first thing I did was go to fetch the kitten. A rather surly man told me without explanation that it had died. It occurred to me that the kitten might have died of neglect, or that they might have sold it because it was a pedigree Persian, but I didn't think at the time of asking any questions. I went up to the top deck of a bus which was luckily empty, and cried all the way back to Langham Street.

The other thing which spoilt my peace in the flat was the owner, who had obviously heard rumours about me and was determined to get me out. She called at unexpected times, hoping to find an excuse to give me notice. One morning she came much earlier than usual and was louder and more explicit than she had ever been before. My daily woman, who was called Mrs. Turner and whom I liked very much, overheard what she said. Next day she told me, without looking at me, that she was sorry but she couldn't work for me any longer. She said that her husband had found a job in another part of London and that she couldn't make the long journey back and forth every day. I was pretty sure that it was the husband who had objected but of course I had to pretend to believe what she said.

It was starting to get cold and the idea of staying in that draughty flat without Mrs. Turner appalled me. She lighted fires, got my breakfast in the morning, kept everything spotless, made cucumber sandwiches for tea, and sometimes even prepared a cold lunch for me before she left.

I made up my mind to leave the flat and booked a room at the Carrington Hotel in Bloomsbury, which no longer exists. When I got my first bill I was horrified. I had so little money left after I had paid that I decided to move again. I told myself that anyway a bed–sitting room would be warmer in the winter, and I knew the bed–sitting room routine. Breakfast was always brought up in the morning, though the time it was brought up varied from about half past eight to half past ten or even eleven, it all depended. They would light a small fire in the room and I would huddle under the blankets and wait until it was warm before I poured out the tea, which was by that time stone cold. A scuttle of coal was left outside the door to keep the fire up, and a large tin jug of hot water. Baths could be arranged for, but took a lot of arranging.

I sent my address to Julian and settled down to an almost completely monotonous existence. When I was dressed I would walk to Tottenham Court Road and have lunch in a vegetarian restaurant there. After that my one wish was to get back to my room and sleep, but some remnant of knowing what I ought to do remained and I would take long walks, have tea at some distant place, then walk back again. I would be in bed by nine o'clock. It was astonishing how much I could sleep. I'm sure I slept fifteen hours out of the twenty-four, and I never dreamed. I slept as if dead.

And then it became a part of me, so I would have missed it if it had gone. I am talking about sadness.

I never picked up anybody and no one picked me up. I had lost all interest in my appearance and would often jam on a hat and go out without looking at myself in the glass. In those days, when going to the hairdresser was not such an ordinary thing to do, many women had a little spirit lamp and tongs to curl up the ends of their hair. I decided I wasn't going to do this any more, but there was some methylated spirits left in the lamp and I wanted to put it away empty, so I threw the spirits onto the fire. A flame jumped out of the fire and singed the ends of my eyelashes and the front of my hair. I hardly noticed this.

When I paid the first week's rent I was surprised to see how little money I had left. It had seemed such a large sum but now it was nearly gone and I had done nothing practical about making plans.

My room was on the second floor and one day as I was going out to the vegetarian restaurant I saw a letter on the passage table, addressed to the name I used then (I have called myself so many different names). It did not look interesting so I postponed opening it until I came back. It was one of those cold grey days, a stormy wind blowing. The letter was from a firm of solicitors in Lincoln's Inn Fields, telling me I would receive a certain sum of money every month, and a cheque was enclosed.

It seems to me now that the whole business of money and sex is mixed up with something very primitive and deep. When you take money directly from someone you love it becomes not money but a symbol. The bond is now there. The bond has been established. I am sure the woman's deep-down feeling is 'I belong to this man, I want to belong to him completely.' It is at once humiliating and exciting. (The only time I have seen this described was in an Italian novel by a man writing as a woman.) Even when Julian brought me the money I knew it was not his and that he had been told to do it, the man still cared what became of me and the bond was still there. To get money through a lawyer, stating please acknowledge receipt and oblige, was a very different matter. The name of the solicitors was H. E. & W.

Graves. I thought: graves indeed. It was completely illogical, but I had never in my life felt more hurt or more angry.

I tore out of the house and walked round and round the square in spite of the wind, thinking out the most sarcastic letter I could write, such as: I always knew you didn't love me much, but I never thought you considered me a servant you could pension off, and so on. Or would it be more dignified to tear the cheque in two and send it back without a word? When I went back into the house the landlord reminded me that the rent was due.

I think that at this time I had a complete conviction that I was a useless person and that I could never get a job. The fear of rejection had sunk very deep. After a sleepless night I changed the cheque. What else could I do? Then I went upstairs and wrote: 'Dear ————, thank you for sending me some money but please don't do it again, as it makes me very unhappy.' I went out and posted the letter. The letter box must have been empty because it fell with a thud. I remember standing there thinking, 'But what shall I do? Now what shall I do?'

Next day I went to the theatrical agent who had got me my first job. I was determined not to go back to the chorus on tour but I knew how little hope there was of anything else. He asked me if I had an evening dress and I said yes, I had. He said that he could probably get me a job in a crowd as an extra in a movie. The movies were just starting in England. He asked if I would do that and I said I would. It wouldn't be for some weeks but he would let me know.

It was three weeks or a month before I had an answer to my letter about the cheque. He wrote: 'It makes me very miserable to think of you in London without any money. We thought that perhaps this was the best way of making sure that this never happened.' (I thought, 'We—yes, I thought so.') 'I do beg you to accept this. If you don't you'll make me very unhappy.'

I got quite used to changing that cheque, because you can get used to anything. You think: I'll never do that; and you find yourself doing it.

The first movie wasn't so bad. It was about a man who cheated at cards. We were the crowd walking about, pretending to drink and talk. I have forgotten how it ended. A quite well-known actor played the man who cheated and his wife played the female lead. Once she sat near me, elaborately made up. I thought, 'She must be at least thirty. Fancy bothering to make up when you're as old as that.'

Though very boring, the job was not an impossible one. But the second call found us at the Alexandra Palace. It was a glass place, and most terribly cold. The film was about early Victorian times. We sat around in cotton crinolines and shivered. The girl next to me said that it was nonsense that we had to part our hair in the middle. 'It may suit some people,' she said, 'but it doesn't suit me. I bet some girls in those days parted their hair at the side, no matter what they say.' 'Yes, I expect they did,' I said; and after that it was too cold for anyone to talk. I caught sight of the leading lady and under her make-up she was blue with cold. Her hands, covered with rings, were red and swollen. After some hours I thought, 'This is not for me,' and I never answered the agent's call again. There is something as unstable as water in me, and when things get tough I go away. I haven't got what the English call 'guts.'

One day at the vegetarian restaurant a man sitting at the same table began to talk to me. He said he was an Austrian and that he was very lonely in London. I listened for a bit, then realised that though I saw his lips moving I wasn't taking in a word he said. I said, 'Sorry, I must go now,' paid the waitress on my way out and left without looking back. Poor man, he must have been lonely, to talk to me. I hope he soon found somebody more lively to keep him company. That was my only adventure in all those months. The days went on, it got colder, and then it was Christmas.

I sat in the armchair looking out of the window onto the empty street, for London is always very empty at Christmas, wondering how I would get through the day. The vegetarian restaurant was closed, and I was to have lunch in my room. At about twelve o'clock the landlord—it was a landlord, not a landlady, in that house—knocked. 'This came for you by messenger,' he said. He was carrying a Christmas tree about three feet high. He put it on the table, said, 'Very pretty,' and went out. There was no letter with it, only a card with HAPPY CHRISTMAS, but of course I knew the handwriting. I said aloud, 'Oh, he shouldn't have done that, he shouldn't have done that.' I sat in the armchair and stared at the tree. There were little parcels wrapped in gold and silver all over it. I think there were fairy lights on it. There was everything, even a big silver star at the top. I stared at the tree and tried to imagine myself at a party with a lot of people, laughing and talking and happy. But it was no use, I knew in myself that it would never happen. I would never be part of anything. I would never really belong anywhere, and I knew it, and all my life would be the same, trying to belong, and failing. Always something would go wrong. I am a stranger and I always will be, and after all I didn't really care. Perhaps it's my fault, I really can't think far enough for that. But I don't like these people, I thought. I don't hate —they hate—but I don't love what they love. I don't want their lights or the presents in gold and silver paper. The star at the top, I don't want that either. I don't know what I want. And if I did I couldn't say it, for I don't speak their language and I never will.

There was another knock on the door and the landlord came in. The food was chicken instead of beef, and a bit of cake because it was Christmas. I rather liked the landlord. He had a trim white beard and he lived in the basement. He said he was going out that evening but would leave my supper of a glass of milk and bread and cheese on the ledge outside. On this ledge you also put the dirty plates when you had finished eating, and he'd come up and collect them when he wanted to. He looked at the tree but he didn't say anything about it. He wished me a Happy Christmas and I said 'Happy Christmas.' I said, 'I'll be glad of the milk, I get very thirsty at night.'

'Yes, but don't drink too much milk,' he said. 'Too much milk is bad for you.'

'Oh, is it?' I said. 'I never heard that before.'

'Too much milk is binding,' he said.

'Oh, I didn't know that,' I said.

He turned at the door and said, 'Now, don't you believe a word they say.'

I ate the chicken and the cake, put the dirty plates on the ledge outside, then I picked up the Christmas tree and lugged it downstairs and into the street. A taxi came crawling along. I got into the taxi with the tree and told the driver to go to the hospital for sick children in Great Ormond Street.

Here comes a complete blank. The next thing I remember clearly is being back in my room. The tree was gone and there was a full, unopened bottle of gin on the table. Did I take the tree to the hospital, or had I asked the taxi driver if he had any children, and given it to him? Did I ask him to take me to a place where I could buy a bottle of gin on Christmas Day, or had it been in the cupboard for a long time, unopened? But this is unlikely because I didn't like gin. Anyway, there it was and there I sat, looking at it. I would wait, I thought, until the landlord went out. The people on the floor below had gone out early. The house would be empty, the street would be empty. I sat in the armchair and smoked cigarette after cigarette. There was no hurry, plenty of time. But now I knew what I wanted. I wanted nothing.

I had gone through about half the packet of cigarettes when someone knocked at the door and came in without waiting for me to open it. I didn't recognise her at first, then I remembered that she had been in the crowd in the first film I'd worked in, the one in which the man cheated at cards. During the interminable waits we had talked and had exchanged addresses. She was an artist's model by profession, she had told me, and lived in Chelsea.

I didn't mind her coming. She probably wouldn't stay long, I thought, and there was plenty of time, plenty of time. She was carrying a pair of red Turkish slippers as a present, which she had bought in the Caledonian Market.

'I guessed your size,' she said.

'They fit beautifully,' I said. 'How kind of you.'

She stared at the bottle of gin on the table and said, 'Are you giving a party tonight?'

'Oh no,' I said, 'not a party exactly,' and I began to laugh very loud. I said I'd got the gin because if I got too blue I'd drink the lot and then jump out of the window.

'But, my dear, this isn't the right house,' she said. 'Oh no, it isn't high enough. If you jumped out of that window you wouldn't kill yourself. You'd just smash yourself up, and then you'd have to live smashed up and how would you like that? You must look for a very tall house.'

'I never thought of that,' I said.

'Lucky I came along, wasn't it?' she said. 'Let's have a drink on it.'

By the time we'd had a couple of gins we were both giggling. Everything suddenly seemed funny. She said, seriously, 'You know, what's the matter with you is you live in the most depressing part of London. I really hate Bloomsbury. I wouldn't live here for anything.

You ought to live in Chelsea, as I do; you'd soon cheer up. I don't
live there just because most of the men I sit for do; I really like it. But
you know, it's a shame, a lot of rich sugars are flocking to Chelsea,
they take all the studios. They grab all the studios and the real artists
can't afford them any more. Gosh, if they knew how they were hated
they'd stay away.'

We had some more gin. 'You know,' she said, 'if you like, I could
easily get a room for you. Would you like me to?'

By this time everything seemed so funny I could only giggle: 'Oh
yes, I'd come, why not?' She said she was leaving London for a few
weeks but would post me the address when she got it. After she left
I had some more gin and went to sleep.

World's End and
a Beginning

———————————————◆———————————————

THE ROOM SHE GOT ME was not in Chelsea but in Fulham. 'World's End' was on the buses. The first morning I woke up there it seemed to me the furniture was so like that in the room I had just left that moving hardly made any difference. But the table, which had been in the middle and covered with a cloth, was now pushed directly under the window and was bare and very ugly. I had put my brush and comb on it, and a box of powder, but they looked small and unimportant. I must get some flowers or a plant or something, I thought. I can't bear that table.

As soon as I was dressed I went out and walked down the King's Road. Then I had lunch at a place where the spaghetti wasn't bad and all the tables were decorated with empty Chianti bottles.

After lunch I walked along looking into shop windows. There were still some last dead leaves hanging on the trees. They looked like birds, I thought. I passed a stationer's shop where quill pens were displayed in the window, a lot of them, red, blue, green, yellow. Some of them would be all right in a glass, to cheer up my table, I thought. I went into the shop and bought about a dozen. Then I noticed some black exercise books on the counter. They were not at all like exercise books are now. They were twice the thickness, the stiff black covers were shiny, the spine and the edges were red, and the pages were ruled. I bought several of those, I didn't know why, just because I liked the look of them. I got a box of J nibs, the sort I liked, an ordinary penholder, a bottle of ink and a cheap inkstand. Now that old table won't look so bare, I thought.

It was after supper that night—as usual a glass of milk and some bread and cheese—that it happened. My fingers tingled, and the palms of my hands. I pulled a chair up to the table, opened an exercise book, and wrote *This is my Diary*. But it wasn't a diary. I remembered everything that had happened to me in the last year and a half. I remembered what he'd said, what I'd felt. I wrote on until late into the night, till I was so tired that I couldn't go on, and I fell into bed and slept.

Next morning I remembered at once, and my only thought was to go on with the writing. I'd go out early and get something to eat, I thought, then have the whole day.

The landlady was rather late bringing up my breakfast. She put the tray down and said, 'I must tell you, miss, that the gentleman in the room below has complained about you. He says that you walked up and down all night. He thought he heard you crying and laughing. He couldn't get to sleep until three in the morning, and he says if it happens again he's going to leave. I must ask you not to make a noise again, or it won't be my lodger downstairs who will have to leave.'

I got out of bed and said, 'All right, I'll leave at the end of the week. But now you must get out.' I took her by the shoulders and pushed her through the door. I have never seen a woman look so utterly astonished. She said, staring at me, 'Well, you are a one!' I slammed the door in her face. Instead of going out to get something to eat I wrote all day and made up my bed myself.

Next morning, when she brought up my breakfast, she said, 'You know, dear, you needn't think that you have to leave at the end of the week, but you must understand that I can't have the gentleman downstairs kept awake all night. You won't do it again, will you, dear?'

I said, 'Don't call me dear, I don't like it.'

She stood there, staring at me. 'If you took your shoes off,' she said, 'then he wouldn't have anything to complain of.'

I said, 'All right, I'll take my shoes off, I promise. But you must get out now, I'm very busy.' I made my bed myself and put the tray outside. After that I always took my shoes off and remembered not to laugh or cry too loud.

I filled three exercise books and half another, then I wrote: 'Oh God, I'm only twenty and I'll have to go on living and living and living.' I knew then that it was finished and that there was no more to say. I put the exercise books at the bottom of my suitcase and piled my underclothes on them. After that whenever I moved I took the exercise books but I never looked at them again for seven years.

Leaving England

AFTER THAT I DECIDED to go back to Bloomsbury. I felt more at home there.

I can't say I felt happy or relieved, more as if something had finished and a weight had gone. Almost at once I met a journalist who was called Alan. He said he and a few friends had started a night club, and would I be an honorary member? The place was in Greek Street, I think—somewhere in Soho, anyway. It was a large room with a raised platform at one end and a piano on it. The first night there was Alan, me, the pianist, a girl he'd brought and one other man. We stayed till late but no one came, and we left feeling very glum. But the next night people began to trickle in and soon it was packed every night. It was called the Crabtree. I have read several descriptions of it which all seemed to me rather false, but of course I knew only my own friends, and perhaps a lot went on that I didn't know. The people were mostly journalists or painters. If any writers came, I never met them.

In the books which refer to the Crabtree a girl called Betty May was supposed to be the star, but she wasn't. The star was a very beautiful girl called Lilliane Shelley who was supposed to be a gypsy. Gypsies were fashionable. Augustus John, who sometimes came, was also supposed to be a gypsy. I never met him or had anything to do with him.

Epstein did a bust of Lilliane. She would sing a ridiculous song called 'Sing to me, my little popsy-wopsy' and be wildly applauded. Betty May sang 'Sigh no more, ladies,' and as soon as she started there would be loud boos and shut-ups, but she sturdily took no notice and went on to 'Hey nonny-nonny.'

It was at the Crabtree that I first made up my mind that somehow I was going to leave England. I hadn't the least idea how I was going to do this, as I hadn't saved up enough money to pay my passage to anywhere, but I was quite determined that this was what I would do.

I went to the Crabtree nearly every night and stayed till breakfast time. Then I went to sleep and woke just in time to get ready for the club again. There were night clubs all over London, all sorts, all prices, and all full of a feeling of excitement that I had never known before and people dancing to the Destiny waltz. A man I danced with one night took me for a drive in a hansom cab and asked me to tea the next day. We had Fuller's walnut cake, and between mouthfuls he asked me to marry him. It was an odd, up-and-down engagement. 'I don't intend to pig it, you know,' he told me one day. My own solution to this odd affair was that we should get married secretly and not tell anyone. 'It'd be such fun,' I said. 'Think what fun we'd have.' But he only answered, 'I don't see what would be the good of that.' It was a lovely summer, the summer of 1914.

When I think back to the 1914 war my memory seems disconnected and vague. I got a job in the crowd at a theatre in Shaftesbury Avenue. The play was called *Monna Vanna,* by Maeterlinck, and had been banned for a long time. It was the Godiva story. A besieging general had said that he would spare a city if Monna Vanna would come to his tent without any clothes on. That was why it was banned. Constance Collier played the part of Monna Vanna, and the dress she wore to the general's tent was so long and so voluminous one couldn't imagine anything more decent. The crowd was a very job lot, but included of course a professional actress to understudy Constance Collier. She walked into our dressing room one day and was horrified at our pink and white make-up. 'You are supposed to be starving citizens,' she said. She had very little success. One girl said, '*I'm* not going to make up as a starving citizen, thank you very much.' Though I saw that it was wrong, I followed suit. Royalty came to the first performance and the stage manager said we must be very careful not to stare at them in their box. I stole a look and thought they looked very bored. I don't know who they were.

Once, looking out of the dressing room window, we saw a long procession of young men. Unlike processions now, they had no banners. When I asked who they were I was told they were German students in London who were protesting against the war. I said, 'What war?' In the back of the dressing room someone said, 'It'll all be over by Christmas; what's the use of making such a fuss?' But one of the girls who was a Hungarian said, 'Oh no, it won't be over by Christmas, don't you make any mistake.'

In contrast to that I can remember coming out of the theatre with the man I was on-and-off engaged to, and seeing the news in Leicester Square tube station in large black letters: ARCHDUKE ASSASSINATED AT SARAJEVO. He said, 'That means war.' But in spite of the queues outside the recruiting offices—and there were long queues—the first time it truly dawned on me that we were at war was when I went to the Crabtree one night and found a notice posted up: CLOSED FOR THE DURATION.

I heard of a canteen near Euston Station, started by a Mrs. Colonel Somebody for the use of troops going to France. They wanted volunteer cooks and waitresses. I knew nothing about cooking or waiting but I went and volunteered. The house was horribly depressing. I hated it, and I disliked Mrs. Colonel too. She called us all together —there were six or eight of us—and after perfunctory thanks she told us the rules:

1. None of the men must be allowed into the kitchen.
2. When we brought in the trays we must smile and say good afternoon or good morning as the case might be, but we must not engage in conversation with any of the soldiers.
3. We must not on any account wash the frying pan. 'It ruins a frying pan to wash it,' she said.

She also told us that the soldiers would be sure to say that they were too poor to pay for their orders, and would ask us to settle their bills for them. This was untrue. From first to last not one of the men asked us to pay, or even hinted at it.

As the frying pan got blacker and blacker, so did the bacon and eggs which we cooked in it. At first a lot of the men asked for bacon and eggs and I was ashamed, sometimes, of what we served up. Then a practical woman from Birmingham came to work with us for two days, took one look at the pan, threw it away and went out to buy another. But by that time the news about our bacon and eggs must have spread and the men had stopped asking for them. I would have hated Mrs. Colonel except that I had to remember that she was paying for the whole thing out of her own pocket; and she did bring along tall bottles of coffee which was quite delicious compared to the coffee one usually got. You heated it up, added milk, and there you were. The soldiers soon cottoned on to that and usually asked for coffee and sandwiches— we had a bread-cutting machine so our ham or cheese sandwiches were quite decent-looking. The place was usually packed. It must have been better than the station buffet.

The younger men often looked excited. The older men were more thoughtful and silent; they knew what they were going to. Only one man ever broke the rule about coming into the kitchen. He was hung around with heavy things. I often wondered how they managed to walk with all that weight. The burden was secured by a strap at the back and he walked in to say laughingly that his strap had got twisted, and would we put it right. I was nearest to him and managed to fix it. He gave me an enormous wink, thanked me and went off. I'm sure he did it for a bet. I prayed for him every night but I don't suppose it did much good.

We worked from nine till five. I would come home dead beat and fall into bed. About the middle of 1917 Mrs. Colonel called us all together and informed us that the Euston canteen had been amalgamated with a similar one at St. Pancras. It was thank you and goodbye.

At this time I was living in Torrington Square. I had moved to a house where I was the only English, or pseudo-English, person, because I thought it looked warm. There were three Greeks, something to do with the tobacco trade, and an Italian woman whom everyone called Signorina to her face and Macaroni behind her back. Then there was a family of Belgian refugees, husband, wife and two grown daughters. There was also a South American couple who had something to do with the stage, or with dancing. I used to think that they had all been attracted there by the house's warm look, which was its only good quality.

Our landlady was a fat woman who took a great dislike to me because I was always demanding hot baths. One morning I came down after my bath at a time when most of the other boarders were gathered in the dining room and she began making her usual sarcastic remarks. Why did I keep asking for hot baths? There must be a reason. It was quite easy to guess what the reason was, and so on. I was so used to it that I hardly listened, so I was very surprised when a man called out to her, 'Oh shut up!' It was the Belgian refugee. He smiled at me and pointed to an empty chair beside him. Soon we were talking and I heard all about his family. He wore pince-nez and when he took them off his eyes were very blue. His wife was a pretty woman, a good deal older than he was, and he told me that she could speak no English or French, only Flemish. 'She must be very lonely,' I said, and he said she was, but she looked quite cheerful. He came from Bruges, and I gathered that he had something to do with a university. When they first came to England they had stayed in a large country house. A lot of people took in Belgian refugees at first. When I asked if he liked the boardinghouse he shrugged and said, 'Well . . .' He was lucky and had been given a temporary job at the Belgian Congo Bank. His name was Camille and when the war broke out he had been writing a book about the Japanese Nō theatre, which he hoped to finish one of these days.

Camille became a great friend of mine, and although his wife and I could not talk to each other she was always kind. Every Saturday they gave what Camille called nursery teas. He had probably picked up the term when they were staying in the country house. Madame had made their room astonishingly homely and comfortable, with chintz and bookshelves. The nursery tea would be coffee—I wonder where she got it from—and plates of thick bread and butter, and the room was always crowded with people whom I found interesting: several other Belgians, an Icelandic poet and so on. They were warm and comfortable occasions and I began to look forward to them.

At one of these teas—it was sometime in the late autumn of 1917 —I noticed a young man sitting in a corner who was staring fixedly at me. Camille introduced me. His name was Jean Lenglet. I talked to him and he asked me to lunch with him the next day, or perhaps it was the Monday after, I forget. Anyway there I was in a Soho restaurant with this rather silent young man. Most girls at this time had a silly technique for such occasions. They would look round the restaurant and pick out some middle-aged or elderly woman and proceed to laugh at her. The man was supposed to compare his amusing companion with the woman laughed at, much to his companion's advantage of course. Perhaps this was subconscious but it certainly often worked. In my heart I thought it a rather unpleasant habit, but as everyone else did it I did it too, though half-heartedly. So no sooner were we seated than I looked round for a woman I could joke about. He listened for a bit, then said without smiling, 'I don't see why you're laughing at her. She's an ordinary woman, just like anyone else. Do you know her? Do you know anything about her?' In a burst of frankness I said, 'No, I don't know anything about her. There's nothing to laugh at and I don't know why I did it.' He didn't answer this, and we began to talk about passports.

Before the 1914 war passports didn't exist. You had to have one for Russia or Turkey, otherwise you went where you liked provided you had the money. He told me he was in London on a diplomatic passport. His stay was limited. He was going to Holland to lecture, or so I understood. He told me he was half French, half Dutch, and lived in Paris. 'All this passport business is only because it's wartime,' I said. 'They'll stop it as soon as the war's over.' He smiled a little and said, 'Perhaps, perhaps.'

After lunch we went to a shop called Bichara which sold scents and cigarettes, and there he bought me a hundred scented cigarettes, which then I loved, and a large bottle of scent. I picked up a glass bottle of kohl—as a powder it's dark but it also glitters—and there was a little stick to put it on with. He asked me if I'd like that too. I said, 'Yes, I would.' 'There's a Bichara in Paris too, you know,' he said, 'in the Chaussée d'Antain.' Outside the shop he hailed a taxi. I thought, 'Now, of course, he'll want to kiss me. Well, it can't be helped.' I was very astonished when he turned away to look through the window and asked me questions about various buildings. What was that building? And what was that one? If I knew I told him, and if I didn't I made it up. When we got back to the boardinghouse he thanked me for coming to lunch, shook hands and explained that he had to go off to meet someone. I went up to my room feeling puzzled.

The landlady decided to give us all a party and everyone who had a fancy-dress costume was to wear it. I had—I don't know from when —a Pierrette costume. The landlady got some butter from some- where—each person had only a small ration—and then she came from the kitchen carrying the thinnest chicken I'd ever seen in my life and everyone burst out laughing. Camille put his hand on my arm and said, 'Don't laugh, don't laugh, she's awfully proud of having got that chicken.' After we had eaten somebody danced and somebody sang.

The boardinghouse was really two houses with a sort of cobble- stone passage between them. I was standing near the door when my Dutch-French acquaintance took me by the hand and pulled me into the cobblestone passage. He was very quiet. There was a huge moon overhead. When he asked me to marry him I was at once surprised and not surprised. I said, 'But I thought you told me you have to leave London almost at once.' He said, 'Yes, I've overstayed my time here already. I stayed because of you. I'm not asking you to live with me in London. I'm asking you to live with me in Paris.' It came to me in a flash that here it was, what I had been waiting for, for so long. Now I could see escape. When I said yes, I would marry him, he kissed me —but quietly, carefully as it were. We went back into the room. It was like a dream.

Next day he left London. I told nobody except Camille, but some- how it seemed to spread and I was astonished by the violence of the reaction. I didn't have a word of encouragement or congratulation from anyone. If they didn't treat it as a joke they thought I was stupid.

He wrote to me from Holland and I answered. At first I made up my mind that I would take no notice of the things people were saying, but gradually their disapproval began to weigh on me. Perhaps I would have changed my mind if it hadn't been for Camille. Walking up and down Torrington Square, he laughed at the prophecies of disaster and told me not to take any notice and that English people were stupid about Paris. 'They're jealous,' he said. 'Of course there are good and bad there like anywhere else, and so there are in Lon- don.' Dear Camille, I shan't ever forget him. He was very solid and commonsensical, and if he approved, mightn't all be well?

So when a letter came from someone who I knew didn't care whether I lived or died, a three-page letter warning me of the fate awaiting me if I did such an idiotic thing, I was able to laugh at it.

After the Armistice it was some time before the steamers to Holland ran regularly. It was early 1919 before I was able to book a passage to the Hook. About a week before I sailed I wrote and told the man who had been supporting me for so long that the lawyer's cheque would no longer be necessary. No one can imagine the acute pleasure with which I wrote this. Next day I got a letter by messenger: 'Can you meet me at the Piccadilly Grill tomorrow for lunch? Important.'

We did meet every now and again and I never knew what would happen on these occasions. Would I burst into tears, or would I begin to giggle hysterically as I looked at him across the tablecloth, talking so smoothly?

At one o'clock I was at the Piccadilly Grill. He smiled at me, but looked rather serious afterwards. The meal was over, we were drinking coffee before he said, 'Are you seriously thinking of marrying this man?' I said, 'Yes, I am, most seriously.' He was silent for a bit, then said, 'I hate to say this but I feel I have to. M. Lenglet is not a suitable person for you to marry.' 'But you don't know anything about him,' I said. He said, 'Well, as it happens I do.' I knew that he had worked in the Foreign Office during the war. He said, 'Did he tell you what he was doing in London in 1917?' 'Yes, he was travelling on a diplomatic passport, he told me.' 'Exactly, and he stayed here long after he ought to have gone. Did he tell you that?' 'Yes, he told me that.' 'When he got to Holland he was watched, and he associated with very questionable people. Several of his friends have been arrested. Oh God,' he said, 'I don't know what to do about this. Of course I have no right to interfere in your life. There are several things I can't explain, but if you marry him you'll be taking a very big risk.' I said, 'I like taking big risks, don't you know that?' He gave a little nod. I said, 'I'm going to marry him whatever you say, or anyone else.' 'You've a perfect right to do what you like,' he said. 'Well, come along, we'd better go.'

Outside the Piccadilly Grill he said, 'Well, my dear, goodbye. If anything goes wrong, will you write to me?' I said, 'Yes, I promise.' 'Then goodbye and good luck to you.' He got into one taxi and I into another. It was only in the taxi that I began to cry.

I got onto the Dutch boat at Gravesend. Everything had gone

wrong. The dressmaker who was making a dress for me suddenly increased her charges. I couldn't pay and she kept my trunk. I had only my suitcase with me, with some underclothes, some blouses and the exercise books. Why I clung to those as I did is something that completely puzzles me. I never looked at them, and the idea of showing them to anyone else never entered my head, yet for the next seven years wherever I went, I took them. This is one of the reasons why I believe in Fate. I wore my old black suit, carried my coat over my arm, and that was the lot. Also I had armed myself with a passport although I was convinced that when everything was back to normal it would be useless. It was a rather dreadful old boat and though I wasn't quite seasick, I nearly was.

The boat stopped and we were at the Hook. The girl who had been sharing the cabin with me went on deck with her suitcase. I knelt down and thanked God for getting me away from H. E. & W. Graves and from London. I vowed solemnly that I would never go back whatever happened, whatever happened whatsoever. Then I shut my suitcase and went on deck too.

Paris

IT WAS A LOVELY AUTUMN in Paris. When we sat eating spaghetti in the sun I felt I had got out of prison. Neither of us had any money but that didn't matter. Jean seemed to be able to borrow from his friends, though not large sums. We got a room in an hotel in the rue Lamartine.

It was after spending a night away with one of his friends that I began to think more seriously about the situation. We had a mattress on the floor, a very thin mattress. I hadn't slept at all. I ached all over the next morning. It was after this that I made up my mind that I'd have to get a job of some sort. There were papers at the Rotonde, on long sticks, and I'd look hopefully down the advertisements every day. I preferred the Rotonde to the Dôme; it was quieter. I thought it lovely to be able to sit in peace with a cup of coffee and look at all the papers without being harried or stared at in any way. So unlike London, I thought. In fact it was just this feeling of freedom and the blue sky and the light which made me feel happy and carefree for the first time for so long.

One day I saw an advertisement in the *Figaro* for a young woman to speak English to a family of children. If it had been for a governess I wouldn't have answered, as I didn't feel qualified to be a governess. But I could manage to speak English to a few children, surely. So I plucked up my courage and went to the address given. The tram took me as far as the church of St. Augustin, then I got down and walked down the rue Rabelais, a short street near the Champs Élysées.

I got to know the Richelots' house very well indeed. It was large and seemed to me stately and in some strange way hidden, standing in its stone-paved courtyard without trees. The concierge downstairs directed me to the floor above and a man with a striped apron opened the door to me. I can't remember the room where I first saw Germaine. She was a small, dark woman with a very gentle expression. She told me one day that the family were half Jewish but I didn't notice it at this time. I only felt at once that she was almost as nervous as I was. If I was nervous and sensitive, she was far more so. She had, as it were, tentacles which stretched further than mine. She had just time to say that she was sure I was what they wanted when the sister, Madame Bragadier, the mother of the children, came into the room. She was far more businesslike than her sister, and of course I didn't miss her quick glance up and down, summing me up in my shabby black suit. But she too seemed to take it for granted that I was suitable, and soon she smiled kindly and said she'd introduce me to the children. As I found out afterwards, she was married to a Roumanian.

At this distance of time I can't quite remember the name of the elder boy. I think it was Georges. The little one, who was about five or six, was a very beautiful child. They both had very good formal manners, but I saw a gleam in the younger one's eye which warned me that he was going to be the naughty one. His name was Pierre, but he was called by everybody Pierrot. I cannot remember now if the other two children I was to talk to were there or not. They were Jacques and Jacqueline, and were the children of Madame Lemierre, who lived close by in the rue St. Honoré. The two sisters departed and left me alone with the children. They all spoke English almost perfectly, without a trace of accent, especially the little one, Pierrot.

I read somewhere the other day that you shouldn't teach a child a second language too young, but it seems to me that this is nonsense. I'm sure that the younger they are the more easily they pick up another language and speak it fluently, without any accent.

I'm not sure if the Lemierre children were there the first day or not, but I do remember how undecided I was how to do my job, which obviously had started at once. I asked them if they wanted me to tell them a story. They all clustered round. The only thing that would come into my head was the story of Joan of Arc, and I told it to them. To my amazement they had never heard of Joan of Arc. I was unwilling to believe this, and went on: 'Surely you've heard of Joan of Arc, who chased the English out of France?' They listened politely but very sceptically.

Soon after this I went down to the dining room for an enormous lunch. The dining room was hung with a very beautiful tapestry. Outside the room I noticed a very lovely statue of a wooden Madonna. She was smiling. After, it was explained to me that she was a thirteenth-century Madonna. Apparently it was then that they made the Madonnas that smile. I'd never seen a smiling Madonna before.

It was later on that I got to know the head of the house, old Professor Richelot, who had been a collector of these beautiful things all his life. I didn't at first recognise him as the head of the house. He was a very silent, modest old man, and of course the red ribbon in his buttonhole meant nothing to me. It also confused me that he and his wife sat not at the head and foot of the table, but at the sides, facing one another. I made up my mind that he must be a tutor.

In spite of the tapestries it wasn't a gloomy room, but a stately one. As the long, elaborate meal went on the sisters talked in a very animated way, but never, to my surprise, in French. They spoke German sometimes, sometimes English, and the talk seemed to be mostly about books. In fact, the whole setup bewildered me because I'd never seen anything like it before. What I remember best was the really delicious coffee at the end. The coffee cups were brown and very thin. Somehow I must get coffee cups just like that, I thought, and I did try, but never, of course, succeeded. You could get brown coffee cups easily enough, but they were always thick.

A short flight of steps led from the dining room to a very large room which they called the studio. It was lined with books, and on the tops of the bookshelves, at regular intervals, were the busts of various people—some I recognised, some I didn't. The windows were long and let in so much light and air that, again, there was not a touch of gloom.

I must say here that I was at this time going to have a baby, and it was becoming obvious. But when after the long meal Germaine said, 'Now you must rest,' I was utterly surprised. It was not my idea of how a governess or whatever I was would be treated. However,

Germaine insisted on leading me into another room and seated me in a huge chaise longue. She threw a rug over me and then enquired if I would like something to read. When I said I would, she brought me a book by Dickens, for most of the novels by Dickens were in the bookshelves, in English and in French translation. 'Now try to sleep,' she said, 'now try to sleep.' She left me alone, but of course I couldn't read or sleep. I was too excited and too happy, for I realised at once that I was in a world that was quite new to me.

I was with them for nearly three months, and the routine was pretty much the same all the time.

I could imagine the house wasn't a house at all, but a person, restful and protective. Listening to a piano being played very far off one day, Germaine said that her sister, Madame Bragadier, was one of the best amateur pianists in Paris. It was the sort of music that suited that house. At six o'clock they'd serve a meal for me in the studio, then I'd go back again by tram to the hotel in the rue Lamartine. I was happy because both sides of me were satisfied—the side which wanted to be protected (for I always felt protected in that house) and the side which wanted adventure, strangeness, even risk.

My husband told me he had found a job but he was very vague about what it was, and after a bit I stopped questioning him. There was a little iron balcony outside our room. As he usually brought friends back with him, we would sit on the balcony and drink white wine. They would laugh and tease when I attempted to talk French, which wasn't very well. Jean insisted that when we were together we must speak English. He said it was far more important that he should learn to speak English without an accent than for me to learn French. After some argument I gave in.

Soon it became impossible for me to go to the Richelots' any more. I remember quite well the last time I took the children for a walk up the Champs Élysées. Pierrot was riding in a goat cart. Are there little carriages drawn by goats in the Champs Élysées now, I wonder? The others were walking by his side. I was sitting alone on a bench. Someone passing smiled at me, I smiled back, and suddenly I was happier than I had ever been in my life. There was nothing, really, to make me happy. I had no money, I didn't even know what on earth I was going to do about my baby, and yet suddenly I was perfectly happy on that bench. I've often thought about it and wondered if, perhaps, it was a trick played on women who are going to have babies —a sort of happiness drug.

Of course I have told myself over and over again that I romanticised these people and that house. After all, I was only there from about nine o'clock to about five or six o'clock. I hadn't the least idea of their life in my absence. I really knew nothing about them. I remember one day when robots were being discussed, Madame Bragadier said, 'Imagine having a robot doing up your dress at the back. Those steel fingers! *Quel horreur!*' When you romanticise something or someone, don't you see something, perhaps, which other people miss? Perhaps if I'd stayed longer I'd have found out that they were quite different from what I imagined them to be. But I'm sure I didn't romanticise the house.

Much later in England, shortly after the Second World War, I heard in a hairdresser's that the Germans had taken over the house and stolen everything in it, and I was very sad. I thought of the Madonna that smiled, and said to myself, bitterly, that she smiled just as gently at the thief as she had smiled at me. Then I thought perhaps it was the eternal smile that is the future as well as the past and the present.

My son was taken off to the hospital when he was only three weeks old. It was, I think, the night afterwards that Jean and I had an argument which became very heated. I was extremely anxious that he should be christened. It really seemed to me the most important thing in the world. Jean was an atheist. He said he wasn't going to give his consent to all this hocus-pocus. I was still weak and in the middle of the argument I started to cry. Jean immediately dashed out to buy a bottle of champagne to cheer me up. He came back bringing two bottles and a friend, a girl he knew very well. By the time the first bottle was finished I'd forgotten all my worries. We were all laughing.

The next morning I had a message from the hospital to say that my son had died. They told me exactly when. He was dying, or was already dead, while we were drinking champagne. I went to the hospital, which was run by nuns. The first question I asked was 'Did you baptise him before he died?' The nun answered, 'Yes, they baptise all babies brought to the hospital.' Astonishing how this comforted me, as I had thought that I too was an atheist, or perhaps an agnostic, but I seemed for that time to have gone back completely to my belief

in all I'd been told at the Dominica convent. When I cried it was half
with relief.

The nun I was talking to was kind. I have never understood why
so many people dislike nuns. I've never felt that at all. On the contrary. It was that same week, I think, that Jean got the job as secretary
to Colonel Myaki, one of the two Japanese officers who were part of
the Interallied Commission.

I think it was early in 1920 when the Commission went to Vienna.
There were representatives of Italy, France, a small British contin-
gent and two Japanese officers. The head of the whole show was an
Italian, General Zucchari. When the Commission left for Vienna the
wives and hangers-on weren't allowed to go with them. We had to
wait for several weeks before we got permission to go. So I was left
alone in Paris. I saw Germaine for a while, then the family left for
Brittany. It was because I was so bored and lonely that I again answered an advertisement to talk English. This time to a little boy.

The flat was in the avenue Wagram, and Monsieur and Madame
were still at breakfast when I arrived. She quite startled me. I was
used to the Richelots' completely bare faces, for they wore no make-
up. She, on the contrary, was very much made up and very pretty. She
was wearing a Japanese kimono with a real obi tied around her waist.
Also, she had on Japanese slippers. She seemed to me exactly like the
heroine of *Petite Madame,* a sentimental novel that was very popular
at the time. Her husband fitted in with the picture very well. He was
large and benevolent looking, and soon left, I suppose to go to his
office. Madame (I've quite forgotten their name) seemed to accept
the fact that I'd worked with the Richelots as sufficient recommenda-
tion and she smiled and proposed to take me at once to her son. She
spoke English well, but with a definite French accent. The little boy
was also a complete contrast to the Richelot children. 'He's a little
shy,' she told me. 'That'll get better when he's used to you.'

He was a very thin, solemn little boy, and gave me his hand without
smiling. He had his mother's huge brown eyes. After talking a little,
Madame announced that she had to go shopping and that she'd leave
us to make friends. This proved to be very difficult indeed. It seemed
impossible to coax a word of English out of him. There were some
English children's books in the room, and I asked if he wanted me
to read him a story. He didn't answer, and I took a book down and

read, but he still wouldn't smile. He stared at me, half suspicious, half frightened. At about eleven o'clock a plump, comfortable woman came into the room—his nurse, I suppose—and told me that at this time he always went for a walk in the Parc Monceau. She asked me to be back in time for the *dejeuner,* which was early, about half past twelve, and I said yes, I would be. So we set out hand in hand. He seemed to have gained a little confidence in me.

The Parc Monceau was just round the corner. We sat on a bench, and we talked—or rather he talked—in very French English. In a little while he seemed to become quite relaxed. I told him another story. We walked about a little. He even smiled, and soon he was chatting away, sometimes in French, sometimes in English. I'd say to him, 'Try to say it in English, Jacques.' I began to feel hungry and to look forward to the *dejeuner.* It must be about time, I thought. We walked along to what I thought was the gate we came in by. He chatted away and I felt from his hand that he wasn't frightened of me any more. We turned right out of the parc gates. It was some time before I realised that I didn't recognise the street we were walking in. After a while I knew that we must have gone wrong somewhere. I tried to say lightly, *'Comme je suis bête!* We'd better go back to the parc and start again.' He didn't say anything, but he stopped talking. We walked for some time but the parc seemed to have disappeared and I realised I was in a part of Paris that I didn't know and I could tell by the feel of his hand in mine that he was getting anxious and worried, and soon he began to cry, at first softly, then louder and louder. I thought of taking a taxi, for of course I knew the address in the avenue Wagram, but I stopped because I knew I had no money at all and wouldn't be able to pay for it. He cried louder and louder and the passers-by began to look at us. I still hoped at every turning that I would see a street I could recognise, but I never did. Everything got stranger and stranger.

I realised that I was completely lost, a nightmare feeling. Then I decided that I must take a taxi and ask them to pay when I got to the flat. I signalled to one but instead of getting in, Jacques started to scream louder than ever and wouldn't budge. The taxi driver looked at us both with a very doubtful expression, and all my French had deserted me. I could only say, *'Nous sommes perdus.'* At last he picked up Jacques and deposited him inside the cab. All the way to avenue

Wagram, Jacques cried and shrieked. I tried to pacify him by telling him he would be home soon, soon he would be with Mama again. This had no effect at all. We reached the avenue Wagram, I rang the bell, and the plump woman whom I had seen before answered it and paid the taxi without hesitation. She didn't look surprised.

Inside the flat she put her arms around Jacques and tried to soothe him, and soon he was soothed enough to tell a long story. He spoke so fast that I understood very little. The woman's face became serious as she listened. Two other women appeared and they all knelt around him and looked at me from time to time, very suspiciously indeed. I tried to explain but I could barely think of a word in French by this time, and I did what I usually do when things get sticky. I ran away. I still had my hat and coat on. I had enough money for the metro.

Soon I was back in my hotel. I bolted the door and of course began to cry. Afterwards I pulled myself together enough to write to Madame Whateverhernamewas, explaining what had happened. I also said that I wasn't well enough to go on with talking English to Jacques. Sometimes now I smile when I think there is a middle-aged, or even elderly, man in Paris with an unnecessary hatred of everything English, and vague memories of a thin Englishwoman in black who tried to kidnap him.

Soon the time came for me to set off for Vienna. The Richelots came back to Paris. Germaine lent me some money and came round to help me do shopping. She advised me, however, to wait till I got to Vienna to buy clothes because, she explained, each country has a different way of dressing and it's better to see what other women are wearing before you buy anything. She also informed me that Vienna was very good for clothes, though of course not as good as Paris. So I only bought a check coat, as mine was very shabby. Germaine and her sister both came and saw me off on the Orient Express.

Paris Again

WHEN MY HUSBAND LEFT the Commission we landed up in Paris again without much money. Jean was very depressed, but I persisted in being hopeful. I notice that when things go very badly, I invariably am. It's the long, dead, dull stretches when nothing happens and time is heavy on my hands, as they say; that's what gets me down. So I thought one day that if Jean wrote three articles I would translate them and sell them to some English paper or magazine. I thought of the Continental *Daily Mail* first.

He wrote the articles. One was about a *chansonnier* of Paris before the 1914 war, Aristide Bryant. I thought this very interesting. Each *chansonnier* composed his own songs, words and music, as well as sang them. Another article described a house in the country where he longed to live. I don't remember the third.

I translated them and felt confident. I had brought one pretty dress from Vienna (all the others had been left behind). I put this on and took the articles to the Continental *Daily Mail* office. When I think of how much courage I had then, I realise I must have been a completely different person. There were two men in the office. One eyed me very warily but the other was nice. He looked at the articles and told me that he liked them, but the Continental *Daily Mail* got all its material from the London *Daily Mail,* the only addition being the list of the names of the people staying at various big hotels.

Then I remembered Mrs. Adam. She was the wife of the *Times* correspondent in Paris and I'd met her at a tea party in London. I asked the nicer man if he could give me her address. He said, 'Oh yes, I was playing golf with George Adam yesterday. They live at the rue Taitbout.' The wary one looked disapproving. As I was going through the door, the nice one called me back and said, 'Now, if you were going to Italy, I could arrange a job for you there. How would you like to be correspondent for the *Daily Mail* in Rome?' I thought he was making fun of me. 'But I'm not going to Italy.' He said, 'Oh, it's quite easy really; you just have to find out who's staying at the big hotels. The managers will always tell you. Then we publish the names in the Continental *Daily Mail.*' I said that I thought I wouldn't be much good at that, and anyway I didn't have any intention of going to Italy.

I decided to go straight to the rue Taitbout. This time I was very nervous, as I had only met Mrs. Adam once, and I wondered if she'd remember me. It was a very pleasant flat and I sat on a comfortable sofa while she looked at the articles. Then she said that she thought them good but that they would be difficult to sell to the English papers.

I asked her if she didn't think the article about the *chansonnier* interesting. 'They were quite famous,' I said. She said, 'Yes, of course, but unfortunately, the English are not interested in that sort of thing in Paris. I'll try, but I can't hold out a great deal of hope.'

I explained briefly how I came to be in Paris. While we were drinking tea she asked me, 'Have you ever written anything yourself?' I thought of the exercise books that I'd carried round without having looked at them for years. I hesitated because I still didn't want to show them to anybody. Then I told myself not to be such a fool, all that was finished and I never meant to go back to London. I was now a completely different person. It would be stupid to miss the chance of making a little money. I said, 'Yes, I've got a sort of thing I wrote years ago—a diary, or rather I wrote it in diary form.' 'I'd like to see it,' she said, and I promised that she should have it next day.

She was being very kind to me, I thought. She was a fat, jovial woman who must have been very pretty when she was younger. It felt very nice sitting on a really comfortable sofa again, sipping tea.

But as soon as I was outside the flat I started feeling reluctant to let anyone see what I had written. I did take the notebooks round to the house the next day, but instead of going up to Mrs. Adam's flat on the second floor I left them with the concierge. I thought that Mrs. Adam probably got a lot of manuscripts and letters, and if mine was forgotten, well, that would be fate and would have nothing to do with me.

Next day I had a *pneumatique* saying she liked what I had written and would I come and see her again? When I saw her again she asked me if I'd mind if she typed it and sent it to a man called Mr. Ford Madox Ford, who published a small magazine, *The Transatlantic Review.* She said that Ford Madox Ford had been the brilliant editor of the *English Review,* a London magazine, and that he was famous for spotting and helping young authors. 'You don't mind if I change parts of it in the typing, do you?' she said. 'It's perhaps a bit naïve here and there.' I said no, I didn't mind at all what she did.

I told myself that she was an experienced journalist and must know far better than I did. However, when she showed me the typed manuscript, which she'd called 'Triple Sec,' I didn't really like it. She had divided it up into several parts, the name of a man heading each part. It was sent to Ford. I kept the notebooks, and started looking at them again one day in 1933. I became interested in them and they were the foundation for *Voyage in the Dark.*

The Dividing Line

FOR A WHILE I lived in Amsterdam with my husband, and there I translated *Perversité* by Francis Carco, a job which was arranged for me by Ford. (When the book was published in English it came out under Ford's name, not mine. My agent wrote to ask why this was so. Ford answered that the publisher, not he, had insisted on his name, which had more drawing power.) It was in Amsterdam that I also finished *Quartet,* my first novel.

Then I left Amsterdam and came to London with *Quartet.* The idea was to sell the novel and then go to Paris on my own. I sent the manuscript to Jonathan Cape, the publisher of *Left Bank,* and it was sent back. I had an introduction to Edward Garnett, to whom I took the novel. He said that Jonathan Cape had turned it down because he was afraid of a libel action from Ford. I was astonished to find how alive memories of Ford still were in England; he was still talked about though he had left the country years before. Edward Garnett said Chatto and Windus would publish *Quartet,* and they did.

In London I met a man called Leslie, a reader for Hamish Hamilton, with whom I had a fifty-fifty affair. With some money I got from America for *Quartet* I went to Paris, because I loved Paris and I hated London, and there, in a cheap hotel, I wrote the first half of *After Leaving Mr Mackenzie.* My husband Jean divorced me. I came back to London, married Leslie, and wrote the second half of *Mr Mackenzie.*

It was 1934. I still had some of the old exercise books with me, and picking them up one day, once again became interested in them. They became the foundation for *Voyage in the Dark*. Chatto and Windus turned it down, so it was sent to Michael Sadlier at Constable, who liked the book.

However, it ran into trouble at once. A telephone message called me to his office.

'Why do you end it like that?'

'Because that's the way it must end.'

'You mean the girl dies?'

'Of course; there is no other end.'

'Oh, I don't know; so gloomy; people won't like it. Why can't she recover and meet a rich man?'

'But how horrible,' I said. 'How *all wrong.*'

'Well, then, a poor, good-natured man,' he said impatiently.

'No, I won't change the end. I won't change one single word,' I said, and rushed out of the office, for I was afraid of bursting into tears.

The next morning he rang me and asked me to go back to his office. I did. I said, 'But can't you see that a girl like that would be utterly bewildered from start to finish? She's dying and there's no more time for her as we think of time. That's how she feels, I'm certain.'

'Oh, give the girl a chance.'

So I spent several gloomy weeks trying to think of two or three paragraphs that wouldn't spoil the book, trying to give the girl a chance.

After *Voyage in the Dark* I went back to Paris again for a holiday, alone, in 1938. When I got back to London and Leslie I wrote *Good Morning, Midnight* rather quickly, which was contrary to all my other novels. It was published by Constable, who liked it very much, just before the 1939 war.

For a long time after that I didn't write. Leslie died. I wrote a short story, 'The Sound of the River.' I met Max, a cousin of Leslie's, and married him.

Max was a sweet man. He had a sense of humour, and could tell funny stories. He had been in the Navy. At Malta, he went ashore with a pal one night and suddenly they were accosted by a policeman. The policeman spoke incomprehensibly for a long while, perhaps in Italian, and after a while Max's friend said, 'Oh, balls,' and the policeman said, 'It is not allowed to say balls to the police of Malta.'

   Writing took me over. It was all I thought of. Nothing and nobody else mattered much to me. In fact, I'm certain I was often disagreeable whenever I was interrupted in the effort to get down and shape the flocks of words which came into my head, I didn't and don't know why.

From a Diary: At the Ropemaker's Arms

(While, for a time, I was separated from Max, I lived in rooms above a pub in Maidstone, and there wrote a diary in a little brown copybook. The year was 1947. This is from the diary.)

Death Before the Fact

This time I must not blot a line. No revision, no second thoughts. Down it shall go. Already I am terrified. I have none of the tools of my trade. No row of pencils, no pencil sharpener, no drink. The standing jump.

The Trial of Jean Rhys

Someone told me that after long torture the patient, subject, prisoner, whatever the word is, answers every question with 'I do not know.'

N.B. Be precise. No one told you. You saw it in a film. Naturally.

Did someone perhaps tell you that was true?
No one had to tell me. I know it is true.

Then there are still some things you know?
Yes.
So your first statement was not correct?
No.

(By the way, who is asking these questions? The Counsel for the
Prosecution. And will there be the Counsel for the Defence? I suppose so. And a Judge? I do not know.)

Yesterday at the cinema in the one and threes, watching the usual
thing. Biff. Bang. Why you dirty double-crossing. Bang. Biff. I am so
sick of fights. It is a funny sort of . . . I cannot remember the word.
Anodyne. Lovely lovely word. Anodyne. Sitting in the darkness in the
one and threes. Bang. Biff. Revolver shots. Surrounded by small
boys, infants in arms who wail, fat mothers, old age pensioners. After
a long speech from the screen, small boy, 'I wanna know what the lady
was saying.' Mother, 'Don' know, ducks.' Small boy, 'What was the
gentleman saying, Mum?' Mother, 'You keep quiet or you'll get
smacked.' You can't do this to me. You dirty double-crossing.

Quotations

> *Les plus désespérés sont les chants les plus beaux*
> *Et j'en sais d'immortels qui ne sont que sanglots.* *

It doesn't make me cry any more.
Something that still persists?
Wait, one more.

> You are seeking a new world. I know of one that is always new
> because it is eternal. O conquistadores, conquerors of the Americas,
> mine is an advantage more difficult, more heroic than yours. At the
> cost of a thousand sufferings, worse than yours. At the cost of a long
> death before the fact, I shall conquer this world that is ever new,
> ever young. Dare to follow me and you will see.

Meditations? St. Teresa.
No more quotations. Paul Morand says in one of his books that
English novelists always start with a quotation. The text before the
sermon. I found that witty.

*From 'La Nuit de Mai,' by Alfred de Musset.

Trial Continued

Do you believe in God?
I do not know.
In human love?
Yes.
Still?
Yes.
In humanity?
No.
How can you believe in human love and not in humanity?
Because I believe that sometimes human beings can be more than
themselves.
Come come, this is very bad. Can't you do better than that?
Silence.
*What you really mean is that human beings can be taken over, possessed by
something outside, something greater, and that love is one of these manifesta-
tions. Then, my dear, you must believe in God, or the gods, in the Devil, in the
whole bag of tricks.*
No, that is not what I mean.
Then what?
I cannot say it. I have not the words.
Say.
I cannot.
You must.
It is in myself.
What is?
All. Good, evil, love, hate, life, death, beauty, ugliness.
And in everyone?
I do not know 'everyone.' I only know myself.
And others?
I do not know them. I see them as trees walking.
COUNSEL FOR THE PROSECUTION. *There you are! Didn't take long, did it?*
COUNSEL FOR THE DEFENCE. *Objection!*
VOICE. *Objection sustained.*
DEFENCE. *Jesus Christ said, or is supposed to have said, the Kingdom of God
is within you.*
That's what you meant, isn't it?

Yes. Perhaps. I do not know.

PROSECUTION. *Where is all this leading? What use is it? I suggest that my case is already proved. Members of the jury—*

DEFENCE. *Objection!*

VOICE. *Sustained.*

DEFENCE. *Did you in your youth have a great love and pity for others?*

Yes, I think so.

Especially for the poor and the unfortunate?

Yes.

Were you able to show this?

I think I could not always. I was very clumsy. No one told me.

What?

No one told me anything that mattered—

PROSECUTION. *Excuse, of course! Well, isn't it an excuse?*

It is the truth.

PROSECUTION. *I suppose you will admit that the things that matter are difficult to tell?*

Yes.

Impossible perhaps?

Perhaps, some of them.

DEFENCE. *It is untrue that you are cold and withdrawn?*

It is not true.

DEFENCE. *Did you make great efforts to, shall we say, establish contacts with other people? I mean friendships, love affairs, so on?*

Yes. Not friendships very much.

Did you succeed?

Sometimes. For a time.

It didn't last?

No.

Whose fault was that?

Mine, I suppose.

You suppose?

Silence.

Better answer.

I am tired. I learnt everything too late. Everything was always one jump ahead of me.

The phrase is not 'I do not know' but 'I have nothing to say.'

The trouble is I have plenty to say. Not only that, but I am bound to say it.

Bound?

I must.

Why? Why? Why?

I must write. If I stop writing my life will have been an abject failure. It is that already to other people. But it could be an abject failure to myself. I will not have earned death.

Earned death?

Sometimes, not often, a phrase will sound in my ear clearly, as if spoken aloud by someone else. That was one phrase. You must earn death.

A reward?

Yes.

Any other phrase?

Yes. You will be helped.

You are aware of course that what you are writing is childish, has been said before. Also it is dangerous under the circumstances.

Yes, most of it is childish. But I have not written for so long that all I can force myself to do is to write, to write. I must trust that out of that will come the pattern, the clue that can be followed.

Why is all this dangerous?

Because I have been accused of madness. But if everything is in me, good, evil and so on, so must strength be in me if I know how to get at it.

This is the way?

I think so.

All right, but be damned careful not to leave this book about.

In this place, the Ropemaker's Arms, I have a small sitting room. The feeling is peaceful in the room. Nothing is unpleasant except the black elephants on the mantelpiece. Three big ones, two small. They are not unpleasant either. They are bearable, but very black and mournful, trunks down, against the dark brown wood.

There is a table in the middle with a white cloth on it, a square table. Three chairs stand round it. There is a very comfortable arm-chair, not podgy or shapeless, it's more like a chaise longue with two cushions. There is a tall narrow sideboard. I like this piece of furniture and have often wondered if it is old or good. I expect not; I know nothing about these things. Behind my back, placed diagonally, a china cupboard. It was empty but I have put some things in, my whisky decanter (empty, oh gosh), my Edward the Eighth mug, a blue flowered china jug. The walls are beige, the lino a darker beige. There are three rugs, harmless. Everything is very clean. The window is large, and through it I can see the street, a bit of the house opposite and a big chestnut tree. The small mean streets and houses are very neat. However, the house opposite is not mean to look at. The steps up are white, the door is white, the roof is pointed. On the wall by the window is a picture in a grey frame of a woman in a white blouse, her hair dark, her features small and neat. She makes no difference at all, she too is harmless. Presented by the artist, I should say. Yes, and a low cupboard for food. After some of the places I have been to, this room is heaven. My last landlady was Grand Guignol.

Drawbacks. From three till about half past five the sun shines directly in. It is hot, and when I pull the curtains, which are a not very good red, the light that comes through is ugly, jaded and weary. At this time too the schoolchildren start shouting. There's a school nearby. I am so close to them that it's as if they were near my chair. I don't mind them too much, they are absorbed in themselves and they can't see me through the net curtain. It's a pity that their voices are so hideous. I've always detested cockney voices, right from the word go, yet I know many people who find them fascinating. I do not. For me there is something mean, also something cruel in the sound. That, of course, is because I have been unhappy in London. Still, there it is.

Reflection. Oh, the relief of words. Always like a constant aching, no, an irritation, harsh, gritty, this feeling about England and the English. Disappointed love, of course. Still, I can be annoyed to frenzy at their hypocrisy, their self-satisfaction, their bloody, bloody sense of humour, and stupid, lord, lord. Well, no more of this. This is an English room in an English pub. That is an English tree, and all the books you read are English books. O.K. O.K. That brings me to my bedroom in waltz time.

(The place I live in is terribly important to me, it always has been, but now it is all I have. The table, the chair, the tree outside, my bed upstairs, it is all I have.)

At first I thought my bedroom hateful. It looks onto the pub back-yard and the pub lavatory. There are other backyards, all hung with washing on Monday, Tuesday, Wednesday and all the other days as well. Our backyard displays a hedge of small red roses, too red, too sharp, small bright roses. My room is small and crowded with furni-ture, washstand, dressing table and so on; with my trunk barely room to move. Waking very early in the morning, a fierce glare comes in through the curtains. The bed is so hard that I ache all over. I wake up to thoughts like 'Let perpetual light shine on her.' What a terrible prayer, I will never pray it again. Let perpetual glare shine on her. I wake up to this thought already made, and to the sound of women's voices in the backyard, or rather yards, wake up to despair which changes to frenzied irritation, because one woman starts singing. She sings American songs in an imitation American way, and she is the daughter-in-law of the house. That dreadful sobbing break in the middle of the beat, copied from someone she has heard. O God, I think, stop her. Then I start thinking of English voices. He had a fruity accent, they say—what do they mean by fruity anyway? Anx-ious? Rich? Heavy? I don't suppose they know what they mean. They never know what they mean. Of a Frenchman, 'theatrical.' Why should it be 'theatrical' for a Frenchman to have a French accent? What about you talking French, I want to say. I try to sidetrack myself by finding the right word. Mean? Mingy? Slobbering? No, I've heard French people say the English sound 'throaty,' as if their mouths were full of pebbles. All no good. Then relief, I have read the word in the *Observer* radio critic, Giles Romilly. *Sub-American,* that is exactly right. I can listen now without wanting to scream. You sub-American, you, and all is well. I can relax. Of course, meeting this woman I can see that, as a woman, she is much better than I am. That girl who yowls so horribly is neat, clean, hard-working, she is not pretty but her figure is slim and pretty. She runs lightly up and down the stairs without touching the bannister. Light of foot and heart is she! All the same, I liked her singing 'Underneath the Arches,' that is a fatal song. I shall now get up, dress, and walk to it all day. 'So sing, sing so, and for the ordering of your affairs, sing them too.'

The bedroom is not too hateful to me any longer, and the landlady has got me a feather mattress and I sleep well. I have learned how to pull the curtains so that I can dress without being overlooked. There's a time in the evening when the backyards are empty. It is cool up here and the light is kind. The roses look better, so does the washing. It's quiet and silent, the family are in the pub.

The landlady of this pub I like especially. She is a tall woman but not too fat, and she has a great deal of quiet unconscious dignity. Also, she is kind-hearted. One day when I came in from my obligation walk I saw several books strewn on the table. I was looking at them when she came into the room. I saw at once from her face that she had bought the books. When I thanked her she said there was a stall in the market that sold second-hand books. There was one about Lucrezia Borgia which I think would put me to sleep. Anything to stop me thinking. I don't think the daughter-in-law and the landlady get on very well, but I rather think the landlady will be able to hold her own. Sometimes her son, the husband, sings too. He sings "Twas all over your jealousy, your crime was your mad jealousy. ' This seems to annoy her very much. When I speak of these rooms, and of my landlady and landlord, I touch wood all the time. I cannot believe it is true, something won't go wrong. I am still cautious, wary. That is enough now, now it's time to sleep. The street is noisy, my pleasant sitting room is hot and sticky, the elephants on the mantelpiece loom.

About England and the English

To tie myself to this one theme when today I want to write of light. Light, not glare. Of moments in my life. My life which will so soon be over.

I have not met other writers often. A few in Paris. Ford of course. Even fewer in England. That does not matter at all, for all of a writer that matters is in the book or books. It is idiotic to be curious about the person. I have never made that mistake. Hey, what's all this about? Well, I say to myself, I have to feel my way. And damn badly you're doing it. Start again. It was Jack, who is a writer, who told me that my hatred of England was thwarted love. I said disappointed love maybe.

I swear that looking out of the porthole that early morning in

Southampton, looking at the dirty grey water, I knew for one instant all that would happen to me.

Well, what did you expect?

Not what I saw.

What were you like?

On my next birthday I'd be seventeen years of age. I had lived all my life in Dominica except once. . . . How clumsily I'm writing. Start again. I had left my island once when I was about twelve. I went to St. Lucia, I was a bridesmaid at my uncle's wedding there. We passed Martinique at night. My Aunt B who was my mother's twin woke me to see Trois Pitons. In the morning we were in Castries. A happy time, sun, cocks crowing (there are fer-de-lances here, be careful), a mongoose. My white bridesmaid's dress, my hair is so straight. O God, let me be pretty when I grow up. Let me be, let me be. O God. Mr. Kennaway doesn't think I'm pretty. He is English. His eyes have a look when he stares at me. Not a pretty little girl.

I'm in love with a sweet little girlie, only one, only one.
I meet her each morning quite early, rain or sun, rain or sun.
To work we go walking together,
    just as gay, just as gay as can be.
She's eighteen and I may be twenty, by and by, by and by.
True we've not overmuch money, she and I, she and I.
There's only two flies in the honey.
Just one little girl and me.

Well, that is the only other time I have ever been away. Now I am seventeen, nearly, and there is England, England, England.

Looking back truthfully, were you sad?

No.

Disappointed?

I did not know it.

Then what?

I never once thought this is beautiful, this is grand, this is what I hoped for, longed for.

Was that to be expected?

Then why did I feel it in Paris?

You were older, much older.

So less easy to impress.

Do you mean that you felt fear and dislike at once?

No, that came later. All I felt was—well, I kept going to sleep. Everyone was irritated. I found St. Paul's bare and dull and Protestant, Westminster Abbey too crowded. I was thirsty and asked for iced water. My English aunt was very annoyed. The theatre disappointed me terribly. I'd thought the scenery would be real because I'd heard it was, but I saw the backcloth move. It was only painted.

Later on I learned to know that most English people kept knives under their tongues to stab me. No one told me. No one told me. I had to find out everything. Ten years were wasted before I got away. Ten years from seventeen to nearly twenty-seven can be a long time.

Come, did nothing please you?

Yes, once I saw a very pretty lady in the park. She was as I thought she would be.

Rich?

Yes.

Respectable?

I think so. I am sure. She had that guarded look. I mean protected.

And the men you saw?

Sometimes I saw men in London too. As I passed them in the street I would feel excited and shy because I found them beautiful. I liked the proud way they walked.

Can you remember one?

Yes, I seem to remember one with slanting eyes and red hair.

Red hair?

Yes, a very dark red, a brown red. That is why I am sure he was real for I don't like red hair much. Yet this man in the street in Piccadilly somewhere, I can't remember.

But the place, I hated it. Cambridge too.

Was there nothing you liked?

Yes, Ely Cathedral.

Not King's College Chapel?

No. Not then. I liked the organ.

Not the Backs?

No. Not then. Later on. Not at first. Yes, there was a bridge I liked. I think it was near St. John's College. I think they told me it was a copy of the Bridge of Sighs.

And that is all you can say for England?

Wait. The theatre. The smell of grease paint. I wasn't happy. Passing through Brokenhurst. *I like this place.* A kind landlady in Devonshire. I liked Weymouth. Also Hastings but I cannot remember why. Cold cold cold. Tough beef to eat. The other girls don't like me much but that is not why. The wardrobe mistress detests me. "Aving a baby is 'ell.' I detest her. She makes me shiver. Fat brute. It is after my third tour that it gets tough. The cold the cold the cold. But I am not conquered yet. I do not cry myself to sleep yet.

One day, one day.

I see something great in your hand, something noble. The fortuneteller who came to the dressing room said that. I was pleased but not surprised. I know. But what? How? Where? Oh, I mustn't miss it. I must be ready. But how? How? Next birthday I'll be nineteen. If I miss it? You won't. But if I do?

You see. Too eager.

Yes.

Well, about England?

Sometimes we were taken for rides, drives, whatever you call it. 'I know a man with a car.'

We?

I generally lived with another girl. On tour, with two.

Well?

We'd pass a big house, a lovely garden. But most of all woods, trees, smooth green fields too. Woods and avenues.

Yes?

I recognised them.

From books you'd read?

I suppose so. But it seemed closer than that. I *knew* them. This, this is England. But we only passed by. I had an odd experience. I met a man called Mainwaring. That was his real name. A Colonel Mainwaring who wanted to adopt me.

Adopt you?

So he said.

Adopt you?

That's what he said. He came down to see me several times. He gave me a bracelet for my birthday. A pretty one. I pawned it and got five quid. Sometimes he kissed me, but very gently. He said he'd take me to Italy.

Adopt you?

So he said. I've often wondered.

What happened?

I met the other man and never saw him again or answered his letters.

Well, so?

Well, it was after that I grew to hate London, to hate England.

To fear it, you mean?

Perhaps. But hate it as well. No one was ever kind to me. I knew nothing, nothing. Nothing about myself or other people. Nothing.

But you were not hopeless?

Only because I determined to leave England, I hated it so.

For Paris?

I never thought of Paris. For New York.

How?

Job in the chorus.

What happened?

The 1914 war.

So you left England without a pang?

Not one. I swore that nothing would ever make me return. No hardship. No sadness. Nothing. I should have stuck to that.

Hell and Heaven

The hell of those who seek, strive, rebel. The heaven of those who cannot think or avoid thought, who have no imagination.

Then the question is how do you know they have no imagination? If they have and do what they do, they are indeed damned.

Mea culpa, mea culpa, mea maxima culpa.

Mortal Sins

Pride, anger, lust, drunkenness??, despair, presumption (hubris), sloth, selfishness, vanity, there's no end to them, coolness of heart. But I'm not guilty of the last. All the others.

Venial Sins

Spite, malice, envy, avarice, stupidity, caution, cruelty and gluttony.

I cannot any longer accept all this.
Do you mean that you are guiltless of the venial sins?
Well. Guiltless!

The Cottage

—————————◆—————————

MAX AND I moved to a small cottage outside a village in Devon, which is still my home. It was offered to us by a friend, and I accepted without seeing it, partly because my husband wasn't well and we would be peaceful there. There were four small rooms. It was scantily furnished, and at first I thought it was peaceful. There wasn't much in the sitting room except a desk and a rather good chair in front of the desk. There was a big double bed and a dressing table in the bedroom. By the time I put our armchairs in the sitting room, however, it began to look very crowded. I took a dislike to it then, and lived in the kitchen mostly. And after I discovered that the kitchen was haunted by spiders and mice, the feeling of peace left me. Our neighbours couldn't make us out at all. Instead of getting better my husband got definitely worse, and at last the doctor insisted he should go into hospital. I protested violently against this, but it was useless.

Max died in hospital. I was left completely alone. I spent my time walking up and down the passage in the cottage, afraid of the spiders and the mice, and all the people in the village.

I remember one day I was very tired and went to my bed and lay on it and looked at the light which shone under the door to the passage, and the last lines of *Voyage in the Dark,* the lines which I had been made to cut, came to me. 'And a ray of light came in from under the door like the last flash of remembering before everything is blotted out and darkness comes.'*

---

*Jean Rhys misremembers. She was persuaded or bullied by Michael Sadlier at Constable not to end the book with this sentence, but she managed to keep it in as the first sentence of the last paragraph.

My Day

[*Jean Rhys did not originally conceive of this article as part of her autobiography. It first appeared in* Vogue.]

MY DAY STARTS very early, usually at three in the morning by my bedside clock. I lie with my eyes closed hoping that I'll sleep again, but no dice. On the contrary, I feel very energetic and have to exercise a certain amount of restraint not to bound out of bed, go into the kitchen, make tea, and smoke. But it'll be four hours before the post comes, or the papers. Too long, it'll mean being sleepy all day.

As something like this happens every night, I'm used to it and have an assortment of literature at the foot of the bed. A thriller, a book called *Lo!* which I'm very fond of, full of marvels and wonders, plagues of grasshoppers, mysterious apparitions, disappearances and so on. The author also asserts, to my great satisfaction, that the earth is not round but flat. As Somerset Maugham said, 'We *believe* the earth is round; we *know* it is flat.' Quite so. That applies to a lot of other things. We believe what we have been told, the theory. What we know, we know.

Lo! is for quiet nights. So is the murder story. Not right for when I wake and hear, not the hound of the Baskervilles, as a French critic said of my 'life in remote Devon,' but the wind moaning and groaning round the house. It's astonishing the noises it makes. Sometimes there's a pause, a silence, then a gust so fierce that you're sure the ramshackle place won't stand up to it, the roof will be blown off, the windows shattered. The whole house creaks and rattles. 'Not well built,' as people have said to me with relish. But there is something else, not a creak, not a rattle, not the house or the wind, but a heavy thump that sounds from the next room. 'You ought to get up and look,' I tell myself, but of course I don't. Instead, I reach for my cookery book.

Long ago in the thirties, when I first began cooking at all, I grew interested, discovered that I liked it and wanted to take lessons from a Frenchman in Sloane Street who was supposed to make you into a *cordon bleu* in twelve easy stages. This was laughed at, so I struggled on until one day, by chance, I came upon Marcel Boulestin's book. At once I saw light. How simple, how direct, how easy to understand. With what authority he said: 'Do.' With what subtle irony he said: 'Don't on any account.' I saw my way then and flattered myself I could produce quite good meals.

Then came the war and chaos. I lost my Boulestin and ever since have been trying to buy another. Recently, as I had to start cooking again, I really searched, nothing else would do. The writers always assume that you are cooking for a large family or have gadgets which you haven't, ingredients impossible to buy. None of them had his directness, his simplicity. When one day a friend rang me up and told me that she'd found Boulestin in a second-hand bookshop, I was delighted. The book arrived and it was very thick. I remembered it as a slim paperback. Quality not quantity. The new one was by Marcel Boulestin and a Madame somebody, carefully got up to look very old. The cover, the print, the careful piecing together of various pages, all combined to give the impression that it was published in the early nineteenth century. Talk about ingredients: '*Hachez finement et mélangez une demi-douzaine de cornichons, quelques câpres, quelques échalottes, une cervelle de mouton ou de veau et deux jaunes d'oeuf.*'

But the feeling of the book, the touch of it, is reassuring. I grow peaceful as I read, '*Les côtelettes devront d'abord mariner pendant vingt-quatre heures dans un plat creux. . . .*' I don't think of the nineteenth century as shut in, prejudiced. To me the nineteenth century is a large mango tree, orchids, sun, heaven, hell—which you could avoid —sudden darkness, huge stars.

Sometimes I sleep again. Or read on quietly until five o'clock, when I can get up, make strong tea, relax, smoke, await the light. When I first came to live in the country, when the rest of the house was intolerable, the kitchen was the one place where I could stop feeling anxious and depressed, where the silence was bearable. I can see the sun rise from one corner, the sun set from another. Nothing like the sad, splendid, West Indian sunsets I can remember, but still quite well worth looking at.

When the post comes, the day starts. Sometimes the news is very satisfactory. I'm to be given a tree by Devon County Council. Indeed, they don't say 'tree' but 'trees.' Have I room for 'trees'? How far do the roots spread? I must find out. Wouldn't it be marvellous if I had room for several trees and at last could live in a forest, which has always been one of my ambitions. Later on I can plan a long elaborate meal, my first if I'm hungry. Settle for bread, cheese and a glass of wine, if I'm not. Isn't the sadness of being alone much stressed and the compensations left out?

What happens next depends on the weather. On fine days I feel childishly happy. It takes very little to make me feel happy now, so happy that I jib at doing anything at all, even answering the loud knocks that occasionally thunder on the door. These are women selling brooms, brushes or rugs, or, more often, someone who wants to convert me. Devon is full of ardent sects and their followers, who, once inside, refuse to leave, standing in the passage arguing with me if I am stupid enough to let them in. There are two ways to get rid of them. One is to say that I'm a fervent Catholic, the other, that I'm cooking something which will spoil if I don't watch it. Neither of these excuses is true, but they nearly always do the trick, especially the second one with women. Not always, though. Once two persistent callers carried a large placard which said in black letters: 'Has God deserted humanity?' Something about the smugness of their faces annoyed me, so I said loudly: 'I should have thought it was the other way round,' and saw not only that this had never occurred to them but anyway that it was rank heresy. I shut the door on them at last with great relief.

Then there's Exeter. What to say about Exeter? It's very full, very crowded and must have been a beautiful city once, but they're pulling it down at a great rate and erecting tall cold-looking buildings, technical colleges, and such. What else have I seen there? A West Indian woman (I'm sure she was a West Indian) walking along the street in a hurry. She dragged after her a very carefully dressed little girl. Out of the child's closely fitting white bonnet peered her dark, bewildered, anxious little face. I couldn't forget her for a long time.

Another day I watched an almost completely naked man in the car park tinkering with his car while my driver fumbled with the boot, his parcels, and keys. The man wasn't in the next car, or the next, but the one after that. When for a moment he straightened up and looked round with contempt at the assembled bourgeoisie, his expression was the most arrogant, conceited and self-satisfied I've ever seen. Stevie Smith said something like this: 'It's all very well to talk about the beauty of the human body, but I can think of a whole lot of other things more beautiful.' So can I. Lions, cats, horses. What about hummingbirds, butterflies, even goldfish. Endless.

Now the shops. I can buy vegetables, drink, make-up. 'It's very 'ot, isn't it?' says the driver. And though he always complains whenever there is a patch of blue sky or a gleam of sun, I, too, am glad when we leave the streets behind and get onto a part of the road where tall trees meet overhead and there is a pattern of light and shadow. After the trees, there's a dull bit enlivened by his remarks about bullocks, red earth, 'fine crops,' and so on.

When we're home again, he always says, 'Safe and sound as the ratcatcher's daughter.' I have a feeling of shyness, inadequacy when I pay him. For so long he's carried my parcels, waited patiently while I buy this and that, helped me over difficult places. Once, when I forgot my key, he managed to climb in through a difficult window. Another day we'd crawled along after a flock of sheep for what seemed hours until I began to fidget and say, 'Oh my God, can't they turn off somewhere!' when he said reproachfully: 'They've as much right on the road as we 'ave.' He always knows when it's going to rain; if he puts up a fence, it stays put; if he plants anything, it grows. How can I pay him for all that?

When I first came here, I always left my door open because, after all, I've nothing to steal, and he'd often remark: 'You ought to be more careful. There're a lot of strangers about.' Though I knew perfectly well that he and his wife call people from the next village strangers, his repeated warnings had an effect. Now I always lock up, though thinking sometimes of that very frightening ghost story about the solitary woman who has just turned the key and shot the bolt for the night, when she hears a voice behind her saying: 'Now we are alone together.'

Chronology

1890   Birth of Ella Gwendolen Rees Williams, who was to use several names before she settled on Jean Rhys. There has been confusion about her age because she disliked revealing it. The date 1894, which appears in *Who's Who,* represents a friend's guess. Her passport gives 1890, and a cousin of hers, now dead, once told me that as children they often used to comment on her being 'ten years older than the century.'

1907   Left Dominica to attend the Perse School, Cambridge, where she spent only one term.

1908   Left school for the Academy of Dramatic Art (not then known as RADA because it was not yet 'Royal'). Death of her father. Left the Academy for the chorus line.

1909   First love affair, which lasted eighteen months.

1919   Went to Holland to marry Jean Lenglet.

1920   Birth of their son, William, who died two or three weeks later.

1922   Birth of their daughter, Maryvonne, who survives her.

1923   Jean Lenglet's arrest on a charge of illegal entry into France and of offending against currency regulations while in Vienna. He had obtained a post there in March 1920 with the Interallied Disarmament Commission, and Jean Rhys had spent several months with him there and in Budapest. Jean Lenglet was extradited to Holland.

1927   Met Leslie Tilden Smith.

1932   Divorce from Jean Lenglet. Marriage to Leslie Tilden Smith. Her
        daughter says of the next six years: 'It was agreed that I would stay
        in Holland for my schooling, both my father and my mother provid-
        ing the money. My holidays were spent with my mother—marvellous,
        with everything a child could wish for: books, ballet, music, pan-
        tomimes, circus, in summer camping and caravaning and summer
        places on the Thames. This arrangement continued until the out-
        break of the war, when I chose to go back to Holland.'

1945   Death of Leslie Tilden Smith.

1947   Marriage to Max Hamer.

1952   Max Hamer charged by firm for which he was working for misappro-
        priating funds, and sentenced to six months' imprisonment.

1953   Went with Max Hamer to live in Cornwall.

1956   Moved to Cheriton FitzPaine in Devonshire, where she spent the rest
        of her life.

1964   Death of Max Hamer.

1979   Death of Ella Gwendolen Hamer, Jean Rhys, on May 14.

Bibliography

The following list of her books is given in order of their first publication:

The Left Bank: Sketches and Studies of Present-Day Bohemian Paris, Cape, London, 1927. Those of the sketches in this book which Jean Rhys wished to preserve are included in *Tigers Are Better Looking* (see below).

Postures, Chatto & Windus, London, 1928. Republished by André Deutsch under the title *Quartet,* 1969.

After Leaving Mr Mackenzie, Cape, London, 1930. Republished by André Deutsch, 1969.

Voyage in the Dark, Constable, London, 1934. Republished by André Deutsch, 1967. Based on Jean Rhys's first piece of sustained writing, described in the present book, page 104.

Good Morning, Midnight, Constable, London, 1939. Republished by André Deutsch, 1967.

Wide Sargasso Sea, André Deutsch, London, 1966.

Tigers Are Better Looking, André Deutsch, London, 1968. Stories, including a selection from *The Left Bank.*

Sleep it Off, Lady, André Deutsch, London, 1976.